Jesus Loves Me and My Body Count

.

JESUS LOVES ME AND MY BODY COUNT
    A YEAR OF PRAYER AND SELF-REFLECTION FOR THE MODERN WOMAN.

Jesus Loves Me and My Body Count

AMBER CHASE

Copyright © 2012 Amber Chase, Lillian Getchell
Lilyfire Fitness Publishing
All rights reserved.
ISBN: 979-8-218-56938-9
First Publication December 2024.
All rights reserved. No part of this book may be reproduced in any manner whatsoever without written permission except in the case of brief quotations embodied in critical articles and reviews.
First Printing, 2025

CONTENTS

- Note from the Author — 1
- Dear Reader — 2
- Jesus Sees Me as More than Just My Body Count — 3
- Jesus Loves You and Your Body Count Too — 7
- Seasonal Message for January, February, and March — 8
- January: New Beginnings & Bold Intentions — 9
- February: Self-Love & Relationships — 41
- March: Courage to Let Go of the Past — 71
- Seasonal Message for April, May, and June — 103
- April: Forgiveness & Grace — 104
- May: Ambition, Dreams, & Hustle — 134
- June: Overcoming Insecurities & Embracing Our Uniq — 165
- Seasonal Message for July, August, September — 195
- July: Freedom & Breaking Chains — 196
- August: Authentic Living — 227
- September: Rest, Reflection & Reset — 261
- Seasonal Message for October, November, and Decemb — 292
- October: Fierce Faith in Tough Times — 293
- November: Gratitude & Grace — 326
- December: Redemption & Growth — 359
- Reflection — 394
- What Can a Modern Woman Do? — 396

Note from the Author

My journey has been anything but conventional, yet it is personal which somehow makes my unrelatable adventure comically relatable. And if I had to jot down a catchy lyric to sum up the plot twists, it would probably be "I may be a bad girl, but I'm a real good person." There was a time when everyone around me told me no one would want to start a life with a single mother, a teenage mother labeled a divorcee regardless of the circumstances. These rumors became beliefs which later lead me to explore or ignore my boundaries in both healthy and unhealthy ways.

My life, both before the adult film industry and during has been filled with complicated dualities, wholesome family dinners contrasting with drama or the image of glamour and passion that I mentally packed away like the luggage I carried on LA trips between studies. Who could imagine that the same country girl who believed wedding vows meant she should pray harder for the character to endure the role of a Long-Suffering Wife would also perform in adult entertainment, have complicated messy relationships and find a way to faith.

The realizations about my past that God has given me have inspired me to share the valuable blessings experience guided by faith. It is my hope that these words resonate with women like me who have walked a similar path. Therefore, I'm excited to introduce "JESUS LOVES ME AND MY BODY COUNT: A YEAR OF PRAYER AND SELF-REFLECTION FOR THE MODERN WOMAN."

In this book, I invite you on a journey of self-discovery, healing, and empowerment, blending the spicy adventures in our lives with the grace of faith. Through heartfelt prayers, thought-provoking reflections, and bold art prompts, this journal encourages you to embrace your unique story and navigate your relationship with God, no matter the details of your past.

Dear Reader

As I sit down to write this note, I am filled with a mixture of gratitude, vulnerability, and excitement. I never imagined my journey would lead me to this moment—writing a book that intertwines my experiences in the adult entertainment industry with my faith and personal growth. For a long time, I felt like my past was a burden, something to hide or be ashamed of, and others have tried to reaffirm this notion without knowing much else about me. But through countless reflections, conversations, and moments of prayer, I have come to realize that my journey is not just a story of passionate adventures and whispered gossip; it's a testament to the resilience of the human spirit and the boundless love of God.

When I first embarked on this path, I was searching for more—more meaning, more connection, and more understanding of who I am beyond the roles I played on camera. I wanted to create a space where women like you and I could feel seen, heard, and empowered, regardless of their past. I believe that our experiences, both joyous and painful, shape us into the people we are meant to be, and that God knows our life is not a mistake. This book is a celebration of that journey—a journey that embraces self-love, faith, and the courage to rise above societal judgment.

Throughout these pages, you'll find reflections, prayers, and prompts designed to inspire you to dig deep within yourself. It is my hope that you will use this journal not just as a guide but as a companion on your path to personal growth and spiritual connection. I want you to know that you are not alone in your struggles, and that your past does not define your worth. Through God's love, we can find peace, strength, and inner peace. Thank you for joining me on this incredible journey. I can't wait to see how your story unfolds.

With love and faith, Amber Chase.

Jesus Sees Me as More than Just My Body Count

Before we begin our daily practice, let me paint a picture of what inspired the development of this resource which I've been called to share. I've always loved the spotlight, I'd dance routines for hours, imagining I was on stage. And I admit it is a rush, standing in front of the camera, embodying fantasies and desires. I've spent over a decade perfecting the art of seduction, knowing how to tantalize and tease in ways that leave people wanting more. My life as a Porn star has opened doors to a world filled with passion, excitement, and a parade of lovers that would make anyone green with envy. But what many don't seem to realize is that the thrill of performing is only a fraction of who I am.

The cameras capture the dramatic angles and accentuate the athletic nature of the physical, the glamour, and the allure, but behind the scenes, there's a woman with a rich tapestry of experiences and passions that go beyond the surface. Not many know I was raising my son while I was in college. I earned a Bachelor of Arts in Art History with a minor in Studio Art, simultaneously obtaining credits towards a Bachelor of Science in Anthropology focused on Archaeology, and after graduating, a Master's in Public Administration, all at the same time as producing videos, performing or attending AVN award shows, (which is the equivalent to the Oscars of the porn industry).

Even fewer know that I pursued modeling for the same reason I spent hours on research papers aiming to make honor roll; I was diagnosed with Histiocytosis X Langerhans cell eosinophilic granuloma when I was 25, a rare condition which I believe I have since recovered, but at the time was told to get my affairs in order. It was a sign to get busy living a life full of interest because it is intense being human. I've always had a thirst for knowledge, a curiosity to experience. Honestly, I used the idea of free speech through erotic art and the excuse of finding a "safe space" to explore new physical pleasures to create my stage name and persona: Amber Chase.

One night, on one of my trips to LA, after a particularly intense shoot, I found myself curled up on the couch at a vacation rental, surrounded by textbooks and take-out food, contemplating the duality of my life. The adrenaline from the day had faded, leaving me with a sense of yearning. I couldn't shake the feeling that something was missing.

4

It wasn't the physical pleasure of sex that eluded me; it was a deeper connection—an emotional bond that transcended the thrill of the chase, or the relationship I was in lacking commitment. This was my second long term relationship, a dramatic and quiet negative pendulum swing from my first husband, who in contrast, was uncomfortable at the thought of going to a nude natural hot spring. However, maybe anonymous sex clubs weren't necessarily where I wanted to spend my time either.

As I scrolled through my phone, I noticed a message from an old friend, Sarah. She and I had met years ago in the industry, but our friendship had always been one of those things that flickered in and out of existence, depending on our busy schedules. I shot her a quick message, asking if she wanted to grab drinks. Surprisingly, she responded almost immediately, and within the hour, we were sitting in a trendy bar, reminiscing about the various wild events within the whirlwind of the entertainment industry.

Over cocktails, we talked about everything from our latest projects to our personal lives. Sarah had recently left the industry and enjoying the quiet and slower pace farming. Whereas I was pursuing my passion for painting on the side. Yet, I was still deeply engaged in the adult industry. Listening to her speak about her journey, I felt a pang of envy mixed with admiration. She had traded the chaos of the adult film world for the quietude of a basic farm life, and it suited her.

"Sometimes I miss the excitement," she admitted, swirling her drink thoughtfully. "But what I've found in morning coffee with neighbors is that it fulfills a part of me that I didn't even know was missing."

I realized that while I had built a career on passion, I had neglected other aspects of myself—the passions and dreams that existed beyond the glitz and glamour or the high of academic pursuits and massive research projects. I longed for something more than physicality or validation. I wanted to feel truly seen and understood, not just as a performer, but as a woman with dreams and aspirations. And yes, I was accomplished in many ways outside the business of chasing fame, but so often it didn't matter what other interesting things or good deeds I had done. My past was like a bell I couldn't un-ring from the perspective of so many people, professionally and personally.

5

As we delved into deeper conversation, I began to share my own struggles. "I love my work, but sometimes I feel like it overshadows everything else," I confessed. "There's a part of me that wants to connect on a different level, to explore the deeper meaning of intimacy or even creativity rather than just the physical act of it. And it seems like so many people can't really be there for the other person in the actual moment, like presently connect with one another."

Sarah nodded, her expression one of empathy. "I get that. The adult industry can be exhilarating, but it can also have unintended consequences if you're not careful. We deserve to pursue what makes our souls come alive, not just our bodies."

"But also, our bodies." We said simultaneously laughing and leaning into one another like an inside joke everyone knew.

The conversation sparked something within me. I realized that my time in the adult film industry didn't have to define me. I could embrace my past while also seeking fulfillment in other areas of life. After that night, I made a commitment to myself. I wouldn't necessarily abandon my career, but decided then I would explore other avenues of fulfillment. I used to bake homemade bread, spend hours outdoors, but now my time was structured around late-night booty calls and early morning call times; I wasn't sure how to find balance, but I knew I could.

Then, life took an unexpected turn, in a dramatic fashion the aimless-turned-violent relationship I was in ended. This shift in my life caused me to take a year to focus on independent content creation and college. The bulk of this book was written during this time and the following year. I have only recently had the courage to organize and share this journey, which in many ways has been a rediscovering faith. Somewhere in all the chaos of creating a sense of calm in my life, I reconnected with a fellow performer, someone who understood the nuances of my world and promised the exploration of the world beyond those in the illusion of lights and call times or directors. He was charming, witty, went on long hikes with me, and had a passion for the arts and fashion that mirrored my own.

As we navigated the complexities of our careers together, I found in him a partner who respected my ambitions and celebrated my successes while also helping me see the lessons in failures. With him, I felt free to be myself—both the seductive star and the intellectual woman - and eventually the relaxed wife and vulnerable woman that finds time to write and share this book. We've built a beautiful life together that fans don't really get to see.

Through it all, I learned that my body count didn't have to define me. I could embrace my sensuality while seeking fulfillment in other areas of life. I discovered that Jesus loves me even if I had experienced divorce, and that my past relationships didn't stop me from having a relationship with God. I began to celebrate my desires without feeling the need to fulfill them in every encounter. I discovered that true intimacy isn't just about the physical; it's about being vulnerable, open, and willing to share your soul with another.

Jesus Loves You and Your Body Count Too

Just as I have found fulfillment beyond the lens of the camera, this journal will help you explore the depths of your own soul, cultivating a vibrant connection with yourself and your faith. Each month focuses on themes like self-love, forgiveness, authenticity, and the courage to break free from whatever holds you back, while incorporating reflection on faith.

Whether you're seeking redemption, striving for personal growth, or simply looking to deepen your relationship with God, this journal is designed to guide you on that path.

It's not about shame or judgment; it's about celebrating who you are—spicy adventures and all—while acknowledging the divine love that surrounds you. So, grab your favorite pen, open your heart, and prepare to embark on a transformative journey of self-reflection and spiritual awakening. Let's dive deep together, embracing our stories, finding joy in our experiences, and recognizing that we are all deserving of love, understanding, and grace—regardless of our past.

Seasonal Message for January, February, and March

If you've picked up this journal, you're probably feeling the tug of something deeper—a desire for connection, healing, and growth. Maybe you've walked away from the church or felt like faith just isn't your thing anymore. That's okay. We all have our paths, and each one is uniquely ours, filled with lessons, laughter, and, yes, a few spicy stories that might make your grandmother clutch her pearls.

January: New Beginnings & Bold Intentions

We kick off the year with a bang! January is all about fresh starts and the courage to set bold intentions. Let's be real, starting anew isn't always easy, especially when the weight of our past relationships and experiences can feel like a heavy backpack we can't seem to set down. But in these pages, you'll find prayers and reflections that invite you to shed that baggage. Let's boldly step into this new year, together, as we discover who we truly are—beautiful, flawed, and more than enough.

February: Self-Love & Relationships

Ah, February—the month of love! While the world focuses on romantic gestures and heart-shaped chocolates, we're diving deeper. In February, we're all about self-love and the relationships that shape us. Whether it's the love we have for ourselves or the connections we build with others, it's time to celebrate our journey. Here, we'll explore how to embrace our complexities and cultivate relationships that uplift rather than weigh us down. Get ready to redefine love—starting with the one you have for yourself!

March: Courage to Let Go of the Past

As we move into March, we're channeling our inner warriors. Letting go of the past can feel like climbing a mountain, but you don't have to do it alone. With God by your side and this journal in hand, we'll unpack the emotional weight we carry and discover the courage to release it. This month is about acknowledging where we've been and celebrating how far we've come, all while letting go of the chains that bind us. Together, we'll forge a path forward, one prayer at a time.

January: New Beginnings & Bold Intentions

Start the Year with Purpose: January is all about embracing new beginnings and setting bold intentions. Like I said—starting fresh can feel like climbing a mountain when the weight of past relationships and experiences clings to us like a stubborn backpack we didn't pack but somehow ended up carrying. But these pages are an invitation to lay it all down. Through prayer and reflection, we'll release what no longer serves us and step confidently into the year ahead. Together, let's discover who we are—imperfect, growing daily, and absolutely worthy of the love and life waiting for us.

January 1: Welcome Back (No Lightning Strikes Yet!)
Prayer: "Hey God, it's been a minute... a few years... or a decade. Honestly, I wasn't sure if I could come back to You after all this time, if it would matter. But here I am. No choir music, no church hat, or shiny leather shoes, just me. Help me figure out how to start fresh with You, without feeling like I need to scrub my whole life clean to do it. And thank You for not smiting me for the things I said or did when I was focused on distractions."

Scripture Reference: "His mercies are new every morning." —Lamentations 3:23

Contemplation: What kept you away from God, and what brought you back now?

Daily Reminder: "God doesn't need me to be perfect."

Engaging Prompt: Feel the crisp cool air outside, breathe deeply, and be refreshed.

My Tender Prayer: "Dear God, awaken the sacred feminine within me. Help me feel connected to my essence and embrace the beauty of my being. Amen."

Reflection Prompt: Start the year artfully. What does femininity mean to you? Write or draw what femininity and faith, looks and feels like to you today. Take your time and doodle it doesn't need to be a masterpiece to be meaningful.

January 2: You're Still Here, God? Cool.

Prayer: "Well, God, I showed up again today. That's a step in a decisive direction, right? I used to think that faith was all or nothing. Either one is at Wednesday prayer group and Sunday service, or I was out here on my own. Help me remember that being in relationship with You isn't about rules but about showing up—even if I miss a day (or a week... or however long it has been). Just help me start small."

Scripture Reference: "Draw near to God, and He will draw near to you." —James 4:8

Contemplation: What would it feel like to trust that God accepts that you'll make mistakes in your life, and it still be, ok?

Daily Reminder: "Faith is a daily check-in, not a line at the DMV."

Engaging Prompt: Take five minutes today to sit quietly and talk to God—no fancy dialog or special words required. Just tell Him how you're really doing.

My Tender Prayer: "Lord, guide me as I reconnect with my sensuality in a healthy way and honor the sacredness of my body. May I walk with grace and confidence. Amen."

Reflection Prompt: List or draw three ways to feel more connected to your body.

January 3: No, God Doesn't Hate You for Skipping Church

Prayer: "God, I know I haven't exactly been a regular at Sunday service, but I'm realizing that church isn't the only way to connect with You. Help me let go of the guilt for not having it all figured out. Teach me to find You in the little moments—like sunsets, good coffee, and deep conversations. And if I'm being honest, I'm still not sure about going back to church. Baby steps, right?"

Scripture Reference: "For where two or three gather in my name, there am I with them." —Matthew 18:20

Contemplation: What are some ways you can feel close to God that don't involve a building?

Daily Reminder: "Church is wherever God shows up—and He's already with me."

Engaging Prompt: Text a friend who makes you feel connected and seen. Bonus points if you mention something prayer-related without it feeling awkward.

My Tender Prayer: "God, show me how to express my femininity in ways that feel authentic and true to me. Help me embrace my unique gifts. Amen."

Reflection Prompt: What are three qualities you admire in other women? How can you incorporate those qualities into your life?

January 4: I'm Not a Saint, but I'm Showing Up

Prayer: "Jesus, I've had some wild nights... and not exactly the kind they'd include as a witness to the gospel. But I'm tired of carrying all this shame. Shame, I don't even understand how it could be so heavy. Shame others created for me. Shame that strangers remind me of in odd moments so they can judge me. If You're really as forgiving as they say, I'm going to need You to show me how that works—because I've got a lot to unload. Help me believe that You love me as I am, not as some version of me that doesn't exist yet."

Scripture Reference: "Therefore, there is now no condemnation for those who are in Christ Jesus." —Romans 8:1

Contemplation: What's one wild thing you need to forgive yourself for today? Late nights or walks of shame included.

Daily Reminder: "God's love doesn't require a background check."

Engaging Prompt: Write down the worst thing you're holding against yourself. Then cross it out and write, "Forgiven." and reflect on how your relationship with God helps your know forgiveness.

My Tender Prayer: "Heavenly Father, let me celebrate the unique beauty of my spirit. Help me to see myself through Your loving eyes. Amen."

Reflection Prompt: Write down five things you love about yourself that reflect your feminine gifts.

January 5: God, Are You Sure You Love Me?

Prayer: "Okay God, I know you're supposed to love everyone, but do You really mean me? Like, me-me, every day, even when I'm not even trying? The one with the past that looks like a season of reality TV? If You're cool with all of this, I think I might start believing it too. Help me see myself the way You see me: flawed, sure, but still worthy."

Scripture Reference: "Nothing in all creation will be able to separate us from the love of God." —Romans 8:39

Contemplation: What part of yourself are you struggling to believe God loves?

Daily Reminder: "There's nothing about me that could scare God away."

Engaging Prompt: List five things that make you lovable. If this feels hard, start with, "I have great taste in food/friends/music."

My Tender Prayer: "Lord, help me release any societal expectations that weigh me down. May I embrace my authentic self without fear. Amen."

Reflection Prompt: Imagine if you could let go of unrealistic expectations starting today. How would that feel?

January 6: No More Fake It Until You Make It

Prayer: "God, I've been told faking confidence is a good thing, that will take you where you want to go. So sometimes it seems as if I forgot what real confidence even feels like. Help me build something real faith in You, in myself, and in the plans, you have for me. I don't need to have it all together; I just need to trust that You do."

Scripture Reference: "Being confident of this, that He who began a good work in you will carry it on to completion." —Philippians 1:6

Contemplation: Where in your life do you need real confidence boost, how would it look if you were glowing with self-love and a sense of readiness for whatever comes next?

Daily Reminder: "God's got me covered, even when I don't feel certain."

Engaging Prompt: Do one thing today that scares you just a little bit—like sending that email, making that phone call, or finally telling someone how you feel.

My Tender Prayer: "God, teach me to appreciate my body as a vessel of Your love. Help me nurture it with kindness and respect. Amen."

Reflection Prompt: List three ways you can care for your body today, whether through nourishment, rest, or movement.

January 7: Do I Need to Pray Out Loud, or Nah?

Prayer: "Jesus, praying all alone, out loud feels weird. It's like leaving a voicemail and hoping You'll call me back. But I know I do not have to know the jargon; prayer doesn't have to sound a certain way—it just has to be real. So, here's me, trying. Teach me how to talk to You like a friend, without worrying about saying the 'right' thing."

Scripture Reference: "Pray continually." —1 Thessalonians 5:17

Contemplation: What's your biggest hang-up when it comes to prayer and taking time to fulfill the practice?

Daily Reminder: "God isn't grading your prayers—He just wants to hear from you."

Engaging Prompt: Record a voice memo of you talking to God. Don't overthink it—just say what's on your heart.

My Tender Prayer: "Dear God, grant me the courage to express my emotions freely and authentically. Help me honor my feelings as sacred. Amen."

Reflection Prompt. Call a friend and see where it leads you.

January 8: New Year, Same Me—But with Jesus

Prayer: "God, it's a new year, but I'm still me. However, I'm realizing you never asked me to become anyone else—just to let You walk with me through the mess. So, here I am, flaws and all. Show me how to grow without pretending I'm already fixed. And help me embrace the idea that loving You doesn't mean I have to hate who I used to be."

Scripture Reference: "He makes all things new." —Revelation 21:5

Contemplation: What's one part of yourself that you can accept instead of trying to change?

Daily Reminder: "Self-improvement is great, but self-acceptance is even better."

Engaging Prompt: Write down three things you love about the current version of you—no 'buts' allowed.

My Tender Prayer: "Lord, help me to connect with other women who uplift and inspire me. May our relationships reflect Your love. Amen."

Reflection Prompt: Reach out to a woman who inspires you. What will you say to her to express your appreciation?

January 9: Body Count? God Still Calls Me Beloved

Prayer: "Okay, God. Let's just say my dating history isn't exactly Bible study material. But I need You to remind me that my past doesn't cancel out my future with You. Every experience—good, bad, and 'WTF?'—taught me something, even if I can't articulate what lesson it provided. Help me believe that nothing I've done makes me less worthy of Your love."

Scripture Reference: "While we were still sinners, Christ died for us." —Romans 5:8

Contemplation: How can you show yourself compassion for the lessons learned through past relationships, good times and bad decisions?

Daily Reminder: "God's love isn't transactional—it's unconditional."

Engaging Prompt: Write down one lesson a past relationship taught you. What can you thank God for in that experience?

My Tender Prayer: "God, remind me of the strength found in vulnerability. Help me to embrace my imperfections and share my true self. Amen."

Reflection Prompt: Think of a time when you felt vulnerable. What did you learn from that experience?

January 10: Breaking Up with Comparison

Prayer: "Jesus, comparison is the worst. Whether it's their career, relationships, or trying to measure my worth against other people's highlight reels. Teach me to focus on the life You've given me and the path I'm on."

Scripture Reference: "Each one should test their own actions. Then they can take pride in themselves alone, without comparing themselves to someone else." —Galatians 6:4

Contemplation: Where in your life are you most tempted to compare yourself to others?

Daily Reminder: "Comparison will drop your connection with your joy faster than a slow Wi-Fi connection."

Engaging Prompt: Unfollow or mute one account today that makes you feel 'less than.'

My Tender Prayer: "Lord, help me release the fear of judgment. Let me walk with confidence, knowing I am enough just as I am. Amen."

Reflection Prompt: Reflect on a moment you doubted yourself. How can you shift that narrative to one of acceptance regardless of the outcome?

January 11: God, Am I Allowed to Dream This Big?

Prayer: "God, sometimes I feel like my true exuberance is off putting for some. It's as if I have to tone myself down, like my dreams are too big for someone with my past. But I'm starting to believe that maybe You like the fact that I dream big. Show me how to chase my goals without doubting that I'm worthy of them—and remind me that I don't have to settle for less just because it's easy."

Scripture Reference: "Take delight in the Lord, and He will give you the desires of your heart." —Psalm 37:4

Contemplation: What's one dream you've been afraid to fully believe in?

Daily Reminder: "If God planted the dream, He'll water the garden it grows in with you."

Engaging Prompt: Write down one bold dream you have for your life. Say it out loud, even if it feels scary.

My Tender Prayer: "Lord, inspire me to embrace creativity as a form of self-expression. Let my art flow from my heart and spirit. Amen."

Reflection Prompt: Wave to your neighbors, complement a stranger and remember to smile.

January 12: I Can Be Holy and Still Enjoy Life

Prayer: "Jesus, sometimes I feel like faith comes with the expectation of boredom, like I must give up having fun to follow You. But I don't think that's the deal. Help me find joy in the things You created me to love—whether that's a good meal with friends, a dance party, or a weekend getaway. Show me how to live with freedom without letting guilt tag along."

Scripture Reference: "I came that they may have life and have it abundantly." —John 10:10

Contemplation: Do you know what brings you real joy, remember how you once spent your time and how you spend your days now, what has changed?

Daily Reminder: "You don't have to trade fun for faith—God is in it for the joy too."

Engaging Prompt: Do one thing today that makes you feel fully alive and be grateful in the moment.

My Tender Prayer: "God, help me honor my faith as a powerful guide. Teach me to listen to the whispers of my heart. Amen."

Reflection Prompt: Reflect on a time when you followed your faith. How did it guide you?

January 13: Boundaries Are My New Best Friend

Prayer: "God, saying yes to everyone all the time is exhausting—and I've learned the hard way that not everyone deserves access to me. Teach me that 'no' isn't mean, or selfish, or unprofessional; it's healthy. Help me set boundaries that honor both my growth and my peace, even if people don't like it. And remind me that I'm not responsible for managing everyone else's emotions."

Scripture Reference: "Let what you say be simply 'Yes' or 'No.'" —Matthew 5:37

Contemplation: Where do you need to set a boundary, and what's holding you back?

Daily Reminder: "A boundary isn't rejection—often it's protection."

Engaging Prompt: Say 'no' to one thing today, even if it feels uncomfortable.

My Tender Prayer: "Dear God, grant me the wisdom to seek balance in my life. Help me prioritize self-care and rest. Amen."

Reflection Prompt: What does balance look like for you? Write about steps you can take to create more balance in your life.

January 14: God's Timing, Not Mine (Ugh)

Prayer: "Lord, I'll be honest waiting on Your timing is rough. There are things I have wanted, and even now- I want things to happen now. But I know you're not in a hurry, even when I am. Teach me how to trust Your plan, even when it feels like my life is on pause. And help me stop refreshing my inbox as if my impatience affects the outcome."

Scripture Reference: "Wait for the Lord; be strong, and let your heart take courage; wait for the Lord!" — Psalm 27:14

Contemplation: What's something you're waiting on that's hard to trust God with?

Daily Reminder: "You are worthy beyond all measure."

Engaging Prompt: Take one thing off your mental 'worry list' today and give it to God. (For real. Don't take it back in five minutes.)

My Tender Prayer: "Lord, may I find joy in movement, celebrating my body as it flows with life. Amen."

Reflection Prompt: What movement brings you joy? How can you incorporate it into your day?

January 15: God, Can We Not Start the Day with Guilt?

Prayer: "Jesus, I've spent so much time waking up feeling guilty—guilty about things I did, things I didn't do, or sometimes even things I thought but would never do. Can You remind me that guilt isn't healthy and isn't from You? Help me to distinguish between Your conviction and my inner critic on overdrive. I want to start today in peace, not punishment."

Scripture Reference: "Therefore, if anyone is in Christ, the new creation has come: The old has gone, the new is here!" —2 Corinthians 5:17

Contemplation: What's one guilty thought you're ready to let go of, or forgive yourself for having, today?

Daily Reminder: "If it's guilt, it's not God."

Engaging Prompt: Write yourself a permission slip: "I am allowed to _____ without feeling guilty."

My Tender Prayer: "God, help me cultivate a space of peace within me. May I find solace in quiet moments of reflection. Amen."

Reflection Prompt: Spend five minutes in silence. What thoughts arise during this time of stillness?

January 16: The Past Isn't a Life Sentence

Prayer: "God, some days my past feels like it's tattooed on my forehead, or worse that anyone can look it all up online while I'm in line at the grocery store. People talk about moving on, but no one tells you how to do that. Can You help me rewrite the story I've been telling myself? And help me reject the story that others try to narrate with assumptions. I don't want to live like every mistake defines me. Teach me to see my past as a chapter, not the whole book."

Scripture Reference: "Forgetting what is behind and straining toward what is ahead." —Philippians 3:13

Contemplation: What's one way your past has shaped you for the better?

Daily Reminder: "The past is a lesson, not a life sentence, it's just things that have brought you to where you are in your life today."

Engaging Prompt: Write a letter to your past self. Be kind—and maybe a little funny.

My Tender Prayer: "Heavenly Father, guide me to honor my boundaries with grace and strength. Amen."

Reflection Prompt: What boundaries do you need to consider in your life? Write about how you can communicate them effectively.

January 17: It's Okay If I Don't Feel Holy Yet

Prayer: "Jesus, I'm trying to sort this faith thing out, but I still feel far from holy. Like, I've seen the Bible app and all, but help me realize that holiness isn't about being perfect—it's about being true. I'm not polished yet, but I'm here."

Scripture Reference: "Trust in the Lord with all your heart and lean not on your own understanding; in all your ways submit to Him, and He will make your paths straight." — Proverbs 3:5-6

Contemplation: What's one way you've seen spiritual growth in yourself, even if it feels small?

Daily Reminder: "Holiness is a journey, not a performance."

Engaging Prompt: Think about one thing you've done differently since reconnecting with God. Write it down and thank Him for that change.

My Tender Prayer: "Lord, help me celebrate my femininity in all its forms. Teach me to embrace my cycles and rhythms. Amen."

Reflection Prompt: Reflect on a part of your life that represents your femininity. How does it empower you?

January Day 18: Rest Isn't Lazy—It's Holy

Prayer: "God, I've got this hustle-hard mentality ingrained so deep and it surrounds me in my media circles, and I hear it in the voice of my friends, that rest just feels like a guilty pleasure. But if You rested, maybe I should too. Help me release the pressure to always be productive and show me that I can honor You by resting. Today, I want to breathe deeply, nap guilt-free, and just be."

Scripture Reference: "Come to me, all who are weary and burdened, and I will give you rest." —Matthew 11:28

Contemplation: What makes it hard for you to rest without feeling guilty?

Daily Reminder: "Rest isn't a luxury—it's a necessity."

Engaging Prompt: Block off one hour today for rest. No multitasking allowed.

My Tender Prayer: "God, fill my heart with compassion for myself and others. Help me approach each day with kindness. Amen."

Reflection Prompt: Think of a time you were hard on yourself. How can you practice self-compassion today?

January 19: You Don't Have to Earn God's Love

Prayer: "Jesus, I'm so used to thinking love must be earned— and no one wants to be canceled. The message is like we must perform, prove, or persuade in order to be seen. But You're telling me that Your love is just... there. Waiting for me, whether I've crushed it today or barely made it through. Help me stop seeing Your love like it's on a scoreboard. Teach me how to receive it."

Scripture Reference: "Not by works, so that no one can boast." —Ephesians 2:9

Contemplation: Where in your life are you trying too hard to prove your worth?

Daily Reminder: "God's love isn't based on my performance—it's based on His promise."

Engaging Prompt: Write down one thing you believe makes you 'unlovable.' Then cross it out and write, "Still loved."

My Tender Prayer: "Dear God, help me release comparison and appreciate my unique journey. May I celebrate my progress. Amen."

Reflection Prompt: Write down three achievements from the past month, no matter how small. How do they reflect your growth?

January 20: God, Help Me Unpack This Emotional Baggage

Prayer: "Hey God, I've got some bags, sure nice luxury ones, but also emotional ones. I've been carrying them around for so long, I forgot what it feels like to travel light. Can You help me start unpacking? Show me how to let go of what's weighing me down."

Scripture Reference: "Cast all your anxiety on Him because He cares for you." —1 Peter 5:7

Contemplation: What emotional weight are you ready to lay down?

Daily Reminder: "My grandma would say, you can't carry peace if your hands are full of the past."

Engaging Prompt: Write down three things you're carrying emotionally. Then pray about releasing them to God.

My Tender Prayer: "Dear God, thank you for the interests and inspirations I have in my life. May I celebrate my progress. Amen."

Reflection Prompt: The past is just a memory? Our decisions are made today

January 21: God, Can You Help Me Like Me?

Prayer: "God, loving myself sounds cute in theory, but truly liking myself? That might be a challenge. Teach me how to see myself through Your eyes. Help me become someone I don't just tolerate and seek to improve but to celebrate."

Scripture Reference: "I praise you because I am fearfully and wonderfully made." —Psalm 139:14

Contemplation: What's one quality you have that you genuinely like?

Daily Reminder: "God likes me—and every day I'm working on liking me too."

Engaging Prompt: Plan a date with yourself this week. What would bring you joy? Write it down and make it happen.

My Tender Prayer: "God, help me embrace my sensuality as a sacred expression of my being. May I celebrate my desires without shame. Amen."

Reflection Prompt: What does embracing your sensuality mean to you? Write about your feelings and experiences.

January 22: Jesus, Are You Sure You Picked the Right Girl?

Prayer: "Okay God, let's be real. Some days I wonder if You got me mixed up with someone else. I don't always feel like the 'chosen' type. But if You say I'm worthy, I'm going to try to believe You—even if every day is a work in progress. Help me see the good things You've placed in me, even when I doubt I belong on this spiritual journey."

Scripture Reference: "You did not choose me, but I chose you." —John 15:16

Contemplation: What's one way God might be calling you that you haven't acknowledged yet?

Daily Reminder: "God doesn't make mistakes—and He picked you on purpose."

Engaging Prompt: Write a list of three things you bring to the table. Yes, you.

My Tender Prayer: "Heavenly Father, help me cultivate patience with myself as I grow. Teach me to appreciate the journey. Amen."

Reflection Prompt: What area of your life requires more patience? How can you nurture that part of yourself today?

January 23: God, I Need People Who Get Me

Prayer: "Jesus, finding community is hard—especially when I'm not sure I fit in anywhere. I have a life that not everyone can relate to, but I want real connections, not surface-level acquaintances. Can You send the right people into my life? People who love You but won't judge me, who know the struggle is real and still stick around. I'm ready for friendships that feel like home."

Scripture Reference: "As iron sharpens iron, so one person sharpens another." —Proverbs 27:17

Contemplation: What kind of friendships are you craving right now?

Daily Reminder: "God didn't call you to do life alone."

Engaging Prompt: Reach out to someone you've been meaning to connect with. Invite them into your world.

My Tender Prayer: "Lord, help me to find strength in my vulnerability. May I share my story with those who need to hear it. Amen."

Reflection Prompt: What story do you wish to share? How might it empower or inspire someone else?

January 24: Help Me Stop Apologizing for Existing

Prayer: "God, help me understand that I don't need permission to exist or to shine. I'm not too much, and I'm not in anyone's way. Teach me to stand tall in the woman You made me to be."

Scripture Reference: "You are the light of the world. A town built on a hill cannot be hidden." —Matthew 5:14

Contemplation: Where in your life do you feel the need to shrink or apologize?

Daily Reminder: "Taking up space isn't rude—it's just being human."

Engaging Prompt: Write down one area where you've been holding back. What's your first step toward showing up fully?

My Tender Prayer: "Lord, guide me to nurture my body with kindness. Teach me to listen when it needs rest, nourishment, or movement. Amen."

Reflection Prompt: When was the last time you listened to what your body needed? What can you do today to care for it intentionally?

January 25: God, I Want to Trust You, but It's Hard

Prayer: "Jesus, trusting You sounds good on paper, but in real life, in the moment? It's scary. I want to believe You've got me, but it feels comfortable to stay in the driver's seat even if it is reckless. Show me how to lean into You as we round the corners when I want to grip tight and ride wild. Can You help me loosen my grip, just a little?"

Scripture Reference: "Trust in the Lord with all your heart and lean not on your own understanding." —Proverbs 3:5

Contemplation: What's one area of your life where you struggle to trust God?

Daily Reminder: "Faith is letting go, not giving up."

Engaging Prompt: Take one small step today to release control—pray and let God handle it.

My Tender Prayer: "Dear God, help me find beauty in my imperfections. May I see them as part of Your perfect creation. Amen."

Reflection Prompt: What imperfection have you struggled to accept? How can you begin to appreciate it today?

January 26: God's Grace Is Bigger Than My Mess

Prayer: "God, my life can look like a dumpster fire sometimes—everything is fine here [insert nervous laughter]. But You've never walked away from me, even when I've made a mess of things. Thank You for showing up in my chaos. I'm learning that Your grace isn't a Band-Aid; it can be a new beginning."

Scripture Reference: "But he said to me, 'My grace is sufficient for you, for my power is made perfect in weakness.'" —2 Corinthians 12:9

Contemplation: Where do you need to let grace step in today?

Daily Reminder: "God's grace can outshine your biggest mistakes."

Engaging Prompt: Write about a recent moment where you saw God's grace, even if it was subtle.

My Tender Prayer: "Lord, help me to connect with other women in my community. May we uplift and support one another in our journeys. Amen."

Reflection Prompt: Identify a woman in your life you'd like to connect with. What will you do to reach out to her?

January 27: Joy Doesn't Need a Reason

Prayer: "Jesus, I want to learn how to feel joy without everything having to be perfect first. Help me stop delaying happiness until I reach some moving goal post or imaginary milestone. Teach me to find joy in the now—even when things aren't tied up with a neat little bow."

Scripture Reference: "Rejoice in the Lord always. I will say it again: Rejoice!" —Philippians 4:4

Contemplation: What's one small thing that brought you joy today?

Daily Reminder: "Joy isn't a destination—it's a choice."

Engaging Prompt: Do something today just for fun—no agenda, no productivity pressure. Write about how it felt.

My Tender Prayer: "God, grant me the courage to be my true self, free from fear of judgment. Help me embrace my authenticity. Amen."

Reflection Prompt: When do you feel most like your true self? Describe that experience in detail.

January 28: God, Can I Be Bold Without Fear?

Prayer: "Jesus, being bold sounds cool, but also... terrifying. What if people think it's a joke? What if people don't get me? Help me stop asking 'what if' and start stepping into who You've called me to be. Give me the courage to be bold, even when fear is tagging along."

Scripture Reference: "The righteous are as bold as a lion." —Proverbs 28:1

Contemplation: Where in your life is fear holding you back?

Daily Reminder: "Fear doesn't disqualify you—boldness is doing it scared."

Engaging Prompt: Write about one bold thing you want to do this week. Now, make a plan to do it.

My Tender Prayer: "Heavenly Father, may I recognize the divine feminine in every woman I meet. Help me to honor our shared experiences. Amen."

Reflection Prompt: Think of a woman who inspires you. What qualities does she embody that you admire?

January 29: God, I'm Learning to Love My Own Company

Prayer: "Jesus, I used to think being alone meant I was too busy to even be unloved or unwanted. But lately, I'm realizing that solitude can be a gift. Teach me how to enjoy my own company and use this time to deepen my relationship with You."

Scripture Reference: "Be still and know that I am God." —Psalm 46:10

Contemplation: What's one way you can make time for meaningful solitude?

Daily Reminder: "Solitude isn't loneliness—it can be self-love."

Engaging Prompt: Plan a solo date this week—just you and God. Write down where you'll go and what you'll do.

My Tender Prayer: "Lord, help me to create a sacred space for my emotions. Teach me to express them freely and without fear. Amen."

Reflection Prompt: How do you currently express your emotions? Is there a different method you'd like to try?

January 30: God, I Want to Start Fresh, for Real This Time

Prayer: "Jesus, new beginnings sound good, but they're not always easy. I want to leave some things behind, but some of it feels comfortable—even if it is not good for me. Help me trust that You have something better waiting for me. Today, I choose to believe in new beginnings, even if they come with a little discomfort."

Scripture Reference: "See, I am doing a new thing!" —Isaiah 43:19

Contemplation: What's one habit, thought, or relationship you're ready to leave behind?

Daily Reminder: "New beginnings are uncomfortable, but they're the start of something."

Engaging Prompt: Write down one step you'll take today toward a fresh start.

My Tender Prayer: "God, may I celebrate my achievements, both big and small. Help me recognize my worth in Your eyes. Amen."

Reflection Prompt: What is one accomplishment you're proud of? How did it make you feel?

January 31: God, I'm Grateful for the Journey So Far

Prayer: "Jesus, I'm still here—still praying, still growing, still trying a month into this new journey. Thank You for sticking with me, even on the days I wasn't sure I could do this. I'm learning that faith is about showing up, not being perfect. Here's to new beginnings—and to knowing You've been with me every step of the way."

Scripture Reference: "The Lord has done great things for us, and we are filled with joy." —Psalm 126:3

Contemplation: What's one thing you feel more confident about than you did 31 days ago?

Daily Reminder: "God celebrates every step, no matter how small."

Engaging Prompt: Write a thank-you note to God for January—what you've learned, felt, and overcome.

My Tender Prayer: "Dear God, thank You for guiding me on this journey of self-discovery. May I continue to awaken to my sacred feminine expression in action within my life. Amen."

Reflection Prompt: Create a bubble bath experience, soothing sounds, aromas, followed by lotion and relaxation.

February: Self-Love & Relationships

Oh, February—the month of love! While the world is caught up in romantic gestures and heart-shaped chocolates, we're taking a different path this month. It's a time for self-love and for renewing our faith in God as we reflect on the relationships that shape our lives. This February let's explore the beauty of loving ourselves as a blessing and look at the transformative power of our connections with others.

February 1: God, Can We Talk About Self-Love?

Prayer: "Hey Jesus, self-love often feels like a marketing ploy, or the buzzword on a bumper sticker, but honestly, it's harder than it sounds. I've spent so much time criticizing myself that I forgot how to be kind to me. Help me see myself through Your eyes and learn to love this unique and beautiful creation that You call 'me.'"

Scripture Reference: "Love your neighbor as yourself." —Mark 12:31

Contemplation: What's one way you can show yourself love today?

Daily Reminder: "Loving yourself isn't selfish—it's essential."

Engaging Prompt: Write down three things you appreciate about yourself, no matter how small.

My Tender Prayer: "God, teach me to love myself as You love me. Help me embrace my imperfections and celebrate my femininity without having to take on an aggressive approach just to be cool. Amen."

Reflection Prompt: Write a love letter to yourself.

February 2: God, Help Me Set Healthy Boundaries

Prayer: "Jesus, let's be honest boundaries aren't my strong suit. I tend to say 'yes' when I want to say 'no.' Help me find the courage to establish boundaries that honor my needs and protect my peace. I want to love others well without losing myself in the process."

Scripture Reference: "Above all else, guard your heart, for everything you do flows from it." —Proverbs 4:23

Contemplation: What's one boundary you've been meaning to set but haven't yet?

Daily Reminder: "Boundaries are a form of self-love."

Engaging Prompt: Identify one relationship where you need to set a boundary and write out what that looks like.

My Tender Prayer: "Heavenly Father, help me trust that I am enough in Your sight. Release my heart from fear and fill me with confidence in who You've created me to be. Amen."

Reflection Prompt: Reflect on a moment you doubted yourself. How can you shift that narrative to one of acceptance?

February 3: God, Teach Me the Art of Forgiveness

Prayer: "Jesus, forgiveness sounds like harmony in theory, but putting it into practice? I want to let go of past hurts and move forward, but it's hard. Help me understand that forgiveness isn't about them; it's about freeing myself. Give me the strength to release the baggage."

Scripture Reference: "For if you forgive other people when they sin against you, your heavenly Father will also forgive you." —Matthew 6:14

Contemplation: Who do you need to forgive (including yourself) to find peace?

Daily Reminder: "Forgiveness is a gift I give myself."

Engaging Prompt: Write a letter of forgiveness—whether you send it or keep it for yourself.

My Tender Prayer: "God, teach me to let go of the fear of being judged. Help me see myself through Your eyes, full of worth and purpose, and give me the strength to walk boldly in that truth. Amen."

Reflection Prompt: Reflect on a moment you doubted yourself. How can you shift that narrative to one of acceptance?

February 4: God, Help Me Appreciate My Relationships

Prayer: "Hey God, sometimes I get so caught up in my own stuff that.... 24/7 I get caught up in my own stuff that I forget to appreciate the people in my life. Help me to recognize the value of those around me. I want to express gratitude for my friends, family, and even the random souls who make my day a little brighter."

Scripture Reference: "Every good and perfect gift is from above." —James 1:17

Contemplation: What's one relationship you're grateful for, and why?

Daily Reminder: "Gratitude transforms ordinary moments into blessings."

Engaging Prompt: Send a quick message to someone you appreciate. Let them know what they mean to you!

My Tender Prayer: "God, help me cultivate a positive self-image. May I appreciate my body as a beautiful creation. Amen."

Reflection Prompt: Write about a time when you felt truly beautiful. What made that moment special?

February 5: God, I'm Learning to Say 'No'

Prayer: "Jesus, saying 'no' feels like a foreign language to me. I feel responsible, I feel eager to find the solution for their problem even if they couldn't be bothered to do so for themselves. I guess some would say that I want to please everyone, but it's draining. Teach me that it's okay to say no without feeling guilty. Help me prioritize my well-being so I can show up as my best self for others."

Scripture Reference: "Let your 'yes' be yes, and your 'no' be no." —Matthew 5:37

Contemplation: What situation or person do you need to say 'no' to?

Daily Reminder: "Saying 'no' is saying 'yes' to yourself."

Engaging Prompt: Think of a recent time you said 'yes' when you wanted to say 'no.' How would you handle it differently now?

My Tender Prayer: "Dear Lord, guide me to treat myself with kindness and compassion. May I speak to myself as I would a dear friend. Amen."

Reflection Prompt: How do you talk to yourself in moments of struggle? Write down a kind affirmation to use next time.

February 6: God, Help Me Recognize Toxic Relationships

Prayer: "Jesus, I want to be surrounded by love, not rom-com movie love, real love, but sometimes I find myself tangled in toxic relationships. Help me recognize the people who drain my energy or bring negativity into my life. Give me the strength to distance myself from what doesn't serve my growth."

Scripture Reference: "Do not be misled: 'Bad company corrupts good character.'" —1 Corinthians 15:33

Contemplation: Which relationships are weighing you down instead of lifting you up?

Daily Reminder: "I deserve relationships that nourish my spirit."

Engaging Prompt: List one or two relationships you need to reassess. What steps will you take to protect your peace?

My Tender Prayer: "God, help me let go of the need for external validation. May I find my worth in Your love and acceptance. Amen."

Reflection Prompt: What are some ways you seek validation? How can you begin to validate yourself instead?

February 7: God, Teach Me to Love My Flaws

Prayer: "Hey God, I've got a laundry list of flaws and a grocery list of things I'll never become, and a mental list of things I'm not proud of. I want to learn how to embrace my imperfections instead of hiding them. Show me that these quirks make me unique, not unlovable. I'm ready to start seeing beauty in my flaws."

Scripture Reference: "For we are God's handiwork, created in Christ Jesus to do good works." —Ephesians 2:10

Contemplation: What's one flaw you can start accepting as part of your story?

Daily Reminder: "Flaws are just features of my fabulousness."

Engaging Prompt: Write a positive spin on a flaw you typically criticize. How can it be a strength instead?

My Tender Prayer: "Lord, teach me to embrace my flaws as part of my journey. Help me to see them as opportunities for growth. Amen."

Reflection Prompt: Some say our passion is a flaw, but it inspires you to explore your faith deeper, so is it in fact a flaw at all?

February 8: God, I Want to Cultivate Compassion

Prayer: "Jesus, the world can be tough, whether it is the crowded internet or the empty suburb street and it's easy to get jaded. Help me cultivate a habit of compassion for others, especially when I don't agree or understand their choices. Teach me to look beyond my own experiences and extend grace to those who are struggling- Including myself"

Scripture Reference: "Clothe yourselves with compassion, kindness, humility, gentleness, and patience." —Colossians 3:12

Contemplation: How can you show compassion to someone today?

Daily Reminder: "Compassion is a Contemplation of God's heart."

Engaging Prompt: Identify a situation where you can offer compassion. Write down your plan to support someone in need.

My Tender Prayer: "Heavenly Father, may I embrace my inner critic with understanding. Help me transform that voice into one of encouragement. Amen."

Reflection Prompt: Write a dialogue between your inner critic and your inner advocate. What does the advocate say?

February 9: God, I'm Ready for Healthy Love

Prayer: "Hey God, I have goals, ones that should be simple, but don't seem to be in this day and age. I want to experience love that's healthy, supportive, and uplifting. Help me to recognize red flags and celebrate green lights in my relationships. I'm ready to attract the right kind of love into my life—one that aligns with Your vision for me."

Scripture Reference: "Above all, love each other deeply, because love covers over a multitude of sins." —1 Peter 4:8

Contemplation: What does healthy love look like for you?

Daily Reminder: "I attract love that nourishes my soul."

Engaging Prompt: Create a list of qualities you want in a partner. What do you need to embody those qualities yourself?

My Tender Prayer: "Dear Lord, remind me that I am deserving of love and happiness. Help me to open my heart to receive it. Amen."

Reflection Prompt: What does self-love look like for you? Describe how you can incorporate it into your daily routine.

February 10: God, Help Me Love Myself Like You Do

Prayer: "Jesus, if I'm being real, with myself and You, I often struggle to love myself as deeply as You love me. I need Your help to see myself through Your eyes, not the world's, not the comments on the internet. Teach me how to embrace my worth, flaws and all, and remind me that I'm worthy of love simply because I exist."

Scripture Reference: "See what great love the father has lavished on us." —1 John 3:1

Contemplation: How can you practice self-love today?

Daily Reminder: "God's love for me is unconditional, and so should mine be."

Engaging Prompt: Write down one way you can treat yourself lovingly today—no guilt attached.

My Tender Prayer: "God, fill me with self-acceptance and love. Help me celebrate my journey, no matter where I am today. Amen."

Reflection Prompt: What part of your journey are you proud of? Write about how it has shaped who you are today.

February 11: God, Let Me Be My Own Best Friend

Prayer: "Jesus, I want to feel good about myself, truly, not in a judgy way. I want to be my own biggest cheerleader instead of the harshest critic. Teach me how to speak kindly to myself and treat myself with the love I offer my friends. Help me build a strong foundation of self-love that no one can shake."

Scripture Reference: "Encourage one another and build each other up." —1 Thessalonians 5:11

Contemplation: What does it mean to you to be your own best friend?

Daily Reminder: "I am worthy of my own love and encouragement."

Engaging Prompt: Write a letter to yourself as if you were comforting a friend. What would you say?

My Tender Prayer: "God, help me to embrace my desires and passions without guilt. May I pursue what brings me joy. Amen."

Reflection Prompt: What are you passionate about? List three ways you can nurture these passions today.

February 12: God, I Want to Embrace Vulnerability

Prayer: "Jesus, vulnerability feels vulnerable - in other words, risky, and I'm not sure, I might be to risk adverse. But I know that true connection requires openness. Help me learn to embrace vulnerability as a strength, not a weakness. Show me that sharing my truth can lead to deeper relationships."

Scripture Reference: "Confess your sins to each other and pray for each other so that you may be healed." —James 5:16

Contemplation: What's one thing you've been holding back that could foster deeper connection?

Daily Reminder: "Vulnerability is the gateway to authentic relationships."

Art Prompt: if you were to write a poem what would it be about?

My Tender Prayer: "Lord, guide me to set healthy expectations in my relationships. May I protect my energy and well-being. Amen."

Reflection Prompt: What would the poem sound like?

February 13: God, I'm Learning to Let Go of Past Relationships

Prayer: "Jesus, letting go of past relationships feels like an uphill battle. I do not intend to go back, or reminisce, I don't even like to think about some of it. Help me release the pain, the resentment, and the 'what-ifs.' I want to make space for new connections, but I know I need to heal first. Help me trust that You have better things ahead."

Scripture Reference: "Forget the former things; do not dwell on the past." —Isaiah 43:18

Contemplation: What's one past relationship you need to let go of to move forward?

Daily Reminder: "Releasing the past opens the door to new possibilities."

Engaging Prompt: Write a goodbye letter to a past relationship. You don't have to send it—just let it out.

My Tender Prayer: "Lord, help me to practice gratitude for my body. May I honor it with love and care. Amen."

Reflection Prompt: List five things you appreciate about your body. How do these attributes support you?

February 14: God, Love Shouldn't Be Complicated

Prayer: "Hey God, why does love sometimes feel like a puzzle? I want relationships filled with joy, understanding, and laughter—without all the drama and frustration. Help me seek out and nurture connections that are simple and life-giving."

Scripture Reference: "Let all that you do be done in love." —1 Corinthians 16:14

Contemplation: What's one way you can simplify love and connection in your life?

Daily Reminder: "Love is meant to be a blessing, not a burden."

Engaging Prompt: Identify one small, simple way to express love today—toward yourself or someone else.

My Tender Prayer: "God, may I cherish my uniqueness and individuality. Help me celebrate the qualities that make me who I am. Amen."

Reflection Prompt: What makes you unique? Write about how embracing these qualities empowers you.

February 15: God, I Want to Cultivate Gratitude in Relationships

Prayer: "Jesus, I want to nurture an attitude of gratitude in myself and my relationships. Help me see the good in others and celebrate their contributions to my life. I want to be the friend who uplifts, not one who is absent or a downer. Teach me to appreciate every person You've placed in my path."

Scripture Reference: "Give thanks to the Lord, for he is good; his love endures forever." —Psalm 107:1

Contemplation: What's one thing you appreciate about someone in your life?

Daily Reminder: "Gratitude changes the way I see the world."

Engaging Prompt: Write a thank-you note to someone who has impacted your life positively—big or small.

My Tender Prayer: "Dear Lord, grant me the wisdom to recognize toxic relationships even among friendships. Help me prioritize those that uplift me. Amen."

Reflection Prompt: Reflect on your relationships. Which ones nourish you? Which ones drain you?

February 16: God, I'm Learning to Accept Love

Prayer: "Jesus, accepting love can feel like a temptation. I often feel unworthy or unsure. Help me to believe that I deserve to receive love and care just as much as I give it. Show me how to embrace love without hesitation."

Scripture Reference: "We love because he first loved us." —1 John 4:19

Contemplation: What's stopping you from fully accepting love in your life?

Daily Reminder: "I am worthy of love, just as I am."

Engaging Prompt: Reflect on a moment when you felt loved. How can you hold onto that feeling?

My Tender Prayer: "God, help me embrace my sensuality as a gift. Teach me to honor my desires and body with respect. Amen."

Reflection Prompt: What does embracing your sensuality as part of the whole person you are mean to you? How can you express it in a healthy way?

February 17: God, I Want to Practice Patience in Relationships

Prayer: "Hey God, patience isn't my strong suit, I want to know where I stand at all times, especially in relationships. I want things to happen on my timeline, but I know love takes time. Help me cultivate patience, understanding, and grace with others and myself."

Scripture Reference: "Love is patient, love is kind." —1 Corinthians 13:4

Contemplation: What's one relationship where you could practice more patience?

Daily Reminder: "Patience is a sign of love."

Engaging Prompt: Identify a specific action you can take to show patience today—whether in a conversation or a situation.

My Tender Prayer "Lord, teach me the importance of self-care. Help me prioritize my well-being without guilt. Amen."

Reflection Prompt What self-care practices do you currently have? Identify one new practice to try this week.

February 18: God, I'm Learning to Speak My Truth

Prayer: "Jesus, speaking my truth can feel daunting. Do I even have a voice? What would I say? But I want to honor my feelings. Help me find the courage to express myself honestly and respectfully in my relationships. Give me the strength to be authentic, even when it's uncomfortable."

Scripture Reference: "Speak the truth in love." —Ephesians 4:15

Contemplation: What's one truth you've been holding back that needs to be shared?

Daily Reminder: "My voice matters, and my truth is valid."

Engaging Prompt: Practice sharing your truth with someone you trust today. How did it feel?

My Tender Prayer: "Heavenly Father, may I find strength in my vulnerability. Help me to share my authentic self with others. Amen."

Reflection Prompt: When was the last time you felt vulnerable? How did it impact your sense of femininity?

February 19: God, I Want to Laugh More

Prayer: "Jesus, life can seem so completely full of responsibilities, and I often forget to laugh. Help me find joy in the little moments and not take life too seriously. Teach me to create a light-hearted environment in my relationships, where laughter flows freely."

Scripture Reference: "A cheerful heart is good medicine." —Proverbs 17:22

Contemplation: What makes you laugh the most?

Daily Reminder: "Laughter is a gift from God—unwrap it daily!"

Engaging Prompt: Share a funny story or joke with someone today. Make them laugh!

My Tender Prayer: "God, help me to recognize that my worth is not defined by my past. May I embrace my journey with love. Amen."

Reflection Prompt: I am beautiful.

February 20: God, I Want to Love without Conditions

Prayer: "Jesus, loving without conditions feels like a scam with some people, especially when I've been hurt before. It is hard to trust. Help me to extend grace to others, just as you do for me. Teach me that love is an action, not just a feeling, and that it doesn't depend on how others treat me, but that I deserve safety and love."

Scripture Reference: "Love is not self-seeking." —1 Corinthians 13:5

Contemplation: What's one way you can practice unconditional love today?

Daily Reminder: "Love is a choice I can make every day and at any time."

Engaging Prompt: Think of someone you can show unconditional love to today. What's your plan?

My Tender Prayer: "Dear Lord, may I find joy in the little things. Help me appreciate the beauty of the present moment. Amen."

Reflection Prompt: Describe a simple pleasure that brought you joy today. How can you incorporate more of this into your life?

February 21: God, I Want to Build Lasting Connections

Prayer: "Hey God, even though I've spent a considerable amount of my life in a long-term relationship of one kind or another, I'm tired of surface-level relationships. I want to build deeper, more meaningful connections, beyond being in the same proximity. Help me to invest time and energy into the people who matter most. Teach me how to nurture these relationships so they grow stronger."

Scripture Reference: "Two are better than one, because they have a good return for their labor." —Ecclesiastes 4:9

Contemplation: What's one relationship you want to deepen?

Daily Reminder: "Building connections takes time, but it's worth every moment."

Engaging Prompt: Plan a special outing or call with someone you want to connect with on a deeper level.

My Tender Prayer: "God, grant me the courage to be true to myself, even when it's difficult. May I stand firm in my beliefs and values. Amen."

Reflection Prompt: I can be soft and delicate when I feel safe.

February 22: God, Help Me Let Love In

Prayer: "Jesus, I'm ready to let love in—from others and most of all, from myself, but it feels scary sometimes. Help me open my heart without fear of what might happen. Remind me that love is worth the risk, and your love is the safest foundation."

Scripture Reference: "Perfect love drives out fear." —1 John 4:18

Contemplation: What fears are holding you back from letting love in?

Daily Reminder: "Love is the antidote to fear."

Engaging Prompt: Write about a time when you took a risk in love. What did you learn from the experience?

My Tender Prayer: "Lord, help me to embrace my flaws as beautiful aspects of my journey. Teach me to love every part of myself. Amen."

Reflection Prompt: Identify a flaw you've struggled to accept. Write about how it contributes to your uniqueness.

February 23: God, I'm learning to Value Myself First

Prayer: "Hey God, I have given so much of my energy to others. It's time I learned to value myself first before I try to pour into others, fill their cup or carry their water. Help me recognize my worth and prioritize self-care. I want to be a better partner, friend, and daughter, and it starts with loving myself first."

Scripture Reference: "Each one should test their own actions. Then they can take pride in themselves alone, without comparing themselves to someone else, for each one should carry their own load." — Galatians 6:4-5

Contemplation: What's one self-care practice you can incorporate into your routine?

Daily Reminder: "I can't pour from an empty cup."

Engaging Prompt: Make a self-care plan for the week. What will you prioritize to love yourself well?

My Tender Prayer: "Heavenly Father, may I appreciate the journey of self-discovery. Help me to embrace each step with grace. Amen."

Reflection Prompt: Take a cool bath, soak, feel love for yourself and your future experiences.

February 24: God, I Want to Embrace Change

Prayer: "Jesus, change can feel overwhelming, and I have experienced so much change especially in relationships. Help me embrace the changes in my life and understand that they often lead to growth. Teach me to let go of what no longer serves me and trust that you have better things in store."

Scripture Reference: "Behold, I am making all things new." —Revelation 21:5

Contemplation: What changes are happening in your life that you need to embrace?

Daily Reminder: "Change is the beginning of something beautiful."

Engaging Prompt: Write down one change you've been resisting. What would it look like to embrace it instead?

My Tender Prayer: "God, help me to cultivate joy in my life. May I choose happiness and positivity every day? Amen."

Reflection Prompt: What brings you joy? Write down three things you can do this week to bring more joy into your life.

February 25: God, I Want to Practice Mindfulness

Prayer: "Jesus, life moves fast, like a river flowing endlessly in a current unstoppable and I often forget to slow down and appreciate the moment. Help me practice mindfulness in my relationships and daily interactions. Teach me to be present and fully engaged with the people around me."

Scripture Reference: "Be still and know that I am God." —Psalm 46:10

Contemplation: What's one way you can practice mindfulness today?

Daily Reminder: "Being present is a gift to myself and others."

Engaging Prompt: Spend five minutes in silence, just being aware of your surroundings. What do you notice?

My Tender Prayer: "Dear Lord, may I be a source of love and light for others. Help me uplift those around me with kindness. Amen."

Reflection Prompt: Think of a person you want to uplift. What can you do to support them today?

February 26: God, I Want to Love through Conflict

Prayer: "Jesus, conflict is part of being human, it is intense sometimes, but it doesn't always feel fun. Help me approach disagreements with grace and understanding instead of defensiveness. Teach me how to love through conflict and to see it as an opportunity for growth in my relationships."

Scripture Reference: "Blessed are the peacemakers, for they will be called children of God." —Matthew 5:9

Contemplation: Think about a recent conflict—how could you have approached it differently?

Daily Reminder: "Conflict can lead to deeper understanding if handled with love."

Engaging Prompt: Choose one conflict in your life. What steps can you take to resolve it peacefully?

My Tender Prayer: "God, help me to find peace in the chaos of life. May I ground myself in your love and tranquility. Amen."

Reflection Prompt: There is beauty in a wind storm.

February 27: God, I Want to Share My Story

Prayer: "Hey God, I often feel like staying quiet, like my story isn't worth sharing, but I know it's part of my journey. Help me find the courage to share my experiences and lessons with others. I want my story to inspire and connect, not isolate. Show me how to use my voice for good."

Scripture Reference: "We overcome by the blood of the Lamb and the word of our testimony." —Revelation 12:11

Contemplation: What story do you feel called to share with others?

Daily Reminder: "My story matters and can impact someone's life."

Engaging Prompt: Write about a significant moment in your life. How has it shaped who you are today?

My Tender Prayer: "Lord, guide me to recognize my achievements and celebrate my victories. May I honor my growth with joy. Amen."

Reflection Prompt: List three achievements from the past month. How do they reflect your progress?

February 28: God, I Want to Celebrate Love Every Day

Prayer: "Jesus, every day can feel just like Christmas. Love should be celebrated—not just on holidays or special occasions. Help me create a culture of love in my life where I appreciate the little moments and express affection regularly. Show me how to make love a daily practice."

Scripture Reference: "Let us not love with words or speech but with actions and in truth." —1 John 3:18

Contemplation: What small acts of love can you incorporate into your daily life?

Daily Reminder: "Every day is an opportunity to love well."

Engaging Prompt: Plan one small act of love for someone in your life today. It could be a compliment, a surprise treat, or just checking in to see how they're doing.

My Tender Prayer: "Heavenly Father, thank You for the gift of self-love. Help me to share that love with others. Amen."

Reflection Prompt: Reflect on how self-love can improve your relationships. How can you encourage others to love themselves?

February 29: God, I'm Grateful for My Journey (Leap Year)

Prayer: "Hey God, as February comes to a close, I want to take a moment to reflect on my journey. Thank You for every lesson, relationship, and challenge that has shaped me. Help me carry these experiences forward with gratitude and wisdom."

Scripture Reference: "In everything give thanks; for this is the will of God." —1 Thessalonians 5:18

Contemplation: What are you most grateful for this month?

Daily Reminder: "Gratitude shifts my perspective."

Engaging Prompt: Write down three lessons you've learned in February. How will you carry these lessons into March?

My Tender Prayer: "God, help me to forgive myself for past mistakes. Teach me to let go and move forward with love. Amen."

Reflection Prompt: Write about something you need to forgive yourself for. What would it feel like to release that burden today?

March: Courage to Let Go of the Past

March is calling us to step into the fierce, fearless women God created us to be. Letting go of the past isn't always easy—it can feel heavy, like carrying a load uphill—but you don't have to carry it alone. With God holding your hand and this journal by your side, we'll gently unpack the emotions we've held onto and find the courage to release them. This month is about reflecting on where we've been, celebrating how far we've come, and breaking free from anything that no longer serves us. Together, through prayer and contemplation, we'll step boldly into the future God has waiting for us.

March 1: God, Help Me Embrace Change

Prayer: "Hey God, change, self-improvement, new directions it all feels like that one ex that you can't quite shake—uncomfortable but necessary. Help me to embrace change in my life without holding onto what no longer serves me. I want to be brave enough to let go and trust that You have something better for me."

Scripture Reference: "No one puts new wine into old wineskins. Otherwise, the wine will burst the skins, and both the wine and the skins are destroyed. But new wine is for fresh wineskins." —Mark 2:22

Contemplation: What change are you resisting that you need to embrace?

Daily Reminder: "Letting go creates space for new beginnings."

Engaging Prompt: Write down one thing you need to let go of this month. How will you start the process? What will you do with the free time you acquire in the process?

My Tender Prayer: "Heavenly Father, thank You for this body I live in. Help me see it as a temple—worthy, sacred, and beautiful. Amen."

Reflection Prompt: List three things you love about your body. If you feel comfortable, sketch or visualize these features with appreciation.

March 2: God, I Want to Forgive Myself

Prayer: "Jesus, forgiving myself is often harder than forgiving others. Help me to release the guilt and shame I've carried. I want to remember that Your grace covers all my mistakes, and I am worthy of forgiveness."

Scripture Reference: "If we confess our sins, he is faithful and just and will forgive us our sins." —1 John 1:9

Contemplation: What's one thing you need to forgive yourself for?

Daily Reminder: "I am worthy of the same forgiveness I extend to others."

Engaging Prompt: Write a letter to yourself expressing forgiveness. What do you need to let go of?

My Tender Prayer: "Lord, I ask again, guide me to nurture my body with kindness. Teach me to listen when it needs rest, nourishment, or movement. Amen."

Reflection Prompt: Are you really listening to what your body needs? What can you do today to care for it intentionally?

March 3: God, I Want to Let Go of Regret

Prayer: "Hey God, regret feels like that nagging friend who won't leave. Help me to release regrets about my past relationships and decisions. Remind me that every experience has shaped me into who I am today, and I can choose to move forward."

Scripture Reference: "Forget the former things; do not dwell on the past." —Isaiah 43:18

Contemplation: What regrets are holding you back?

Daily Reminder: "Regret is a thief of joy; I choose to move forward."

Engaging Prompt: List three lessons you've learned from your past that you can appreciate instead of regretting.

My Tender Prayer: "God, remind me again, please help me embrace my body's uniqueness. May I celebrate its differences and appreciate its strengths, and maybe help me be more consistent with my fitness routine. Amen."

Reflection Prompt: Ask yourself again, what do you love most about your body's uniqueness? Write about how it contributes to your identity.

March 4: God, I Want to Release Toxic Relationships

Prayer: "Jesus, I know it is just a metaphor, but some relationships are like old shoes—worn out and uncomfortable. Help me have the courage to let go of toxic connections even if they are beneficial to my bank account or social circle. If they drain my energy and joy, it's time to recycle the worn-out patterns. I want to surround myself with those who uplift and inspire me."

Scripture Reference: "Do not be misled: 'Bad company corrupts good character.'" —1 Corinthians 15:33

Contemplation: Which relationships are no longer serving your well-being, including friendships?

Daily Reminder: "Surrounding myself with positivity brings me peace."

Engaging Prompt: Identify one toxic relationship to distance yourself from - even if it is just a relationship with an IDEA. What's your first step?

My Tender Prayer: "Dear Lord, help me appreciate my body for all it does for me. May I honor it with gratitude and love by getting some fresh air outdoors today. Amen."

Reflection Prompt: Write a list of things your body allows you to do each day. How does this awareness change your perspective?

March 5: God, I'm Learning to Accept My Past

Prayer: "Hey God, accepting my past feels like trying to wear a dress two sizes too small—uncomfortable and unflattering or out of style. But my experience is my life I am living. Help me embrace my history, including the mistakes, because they've all led me here. I want to view my journey as a beautiful tapestry of growth."

Scripture Reference: "And we know that in all things God works for the good of those who love him." —Romans 8:28

Contemplation: How has your past contributed to who you are today?

Daily Reminder: "My past is a part of my story, but it does not define me."

Engaging Prompt: Write about a moment from your past that taught you a valuable lesson. How has it shaped your present?

My Tender Prayer: "God, help me to let go of societal standards of beauty. Teach me to find beauty in my authenticity. Amen."

Reflection Prompt: What opinions or societal beauty standards have affected your self-image? How can you challenge or redefine them for yourself?

March 6: God, I Want to Break Free from Shame

Prayer: "Jesus, shame can feel suffocating, like wearing a heavy coat in the summer. Help me break free from the shame I've carried from my past. Remind me that I am loved and accepted as I am, and I don't need to hide behind what others perceive as my mistakes."

Scripture Reference: "There is now no condemnation for those who are in Christ Jesus." —Romans 8:1

Contemplation: What shame do you need to release to feel freer?

Daily Reminder: "I am loved unconditionally; shame has no place in my life."

Engaging Prompt: Identify one shameful thought or belief about yourself and challenge it. What's the truth?

My Tender Prayer: "Lord, may I find joy in movement. Help me to celebrate my body through exercise that feels good and nourishing. Amen."

Reflection Prompt: What physical activities make you feel alive? Schedule time for one of these activities this week.

March 7: God, I Want to Create Healthy Boundaries

Prayer: "Hey God, healthy boundaries can feel like building a wall, and risking the relationship, but I know they're necessary for my well-being. Help me establish clear boundaries in my relationships that protect my peace while allowing love to flourish."

Scripture Reference: "Above all else, guard your heart, for everything you do flows from it." —Proverbs 4:23

Contemplation: What boundaries do you need to set to protect your heart?

Daily Reminder: "Boundaries are not walls; they are gates that allow healthy love in."

Engaging Prompt: Choose one boundary to establish this week. How will you communicate it to others?

My Tender Prayer: "Heavenly Father, help me to practice body positivity. Teach me to speak kindly to myself and appreciate my form. Amen."

Reflection Prompt: Write down negative thoughts you've had about your body. Now, counter each with a positive affirmation.

March 8: God, I Want to Embrace Forgiveness

Prayer: "Jesus, holding onto grudges or replaying old events in my mind feels like carrying a backpack full of rocks. Help me to forgive those who've hurt me and release the burden. I want to experience the freedom that comes from letting go and moving forward."

Scripture Reference: "Forgive, and you will be forgiven." —Luke 6:37

Contemplation: Who do you need to forgive to find peace?

Daily Reminder: "Forgiveness is a gift I give to myself."

Engaging Prompt: Write down one person you need to forgive. What steps can you take toward forgiveness today?

My Tender Prayer: "God, grant me the strength to treat my body as a sacred space. Help me avoid habits that harm my well-being. Amen."

Reflection Prompt: What habits do you want to change to better honor your body? Outline a plan to start making these changes.

March 9: God, I Want to Trust in Your Plan

Prayer: "Hey God, trusting in Your plan is sometimes like waiting for a text back from a crush—awkward! Help me release my need to control everything and trust that You're leading me toward what's best for me."

Scripture Reference: "For I know the plans I have for you," declares the Lord. —Jeremiah 29:11

Contemplation: What aspect of your life do you struggle to trust God with?

Daily Reminder: "Trusting God is the first step toward peace."

Engaging Prompt: Write about a time when you didn't understand God's plan, but it worked out for the best.

My Tender Prayer: "Dear Lord, help me celebrate the changes my body goes through. May I embrace each stage of my life with grace. Amen."

Reflection Prompt: Reflect on a physical change you've experienced. How has it shaped your self-image or confidence?

March 10: God, I Want to Let Go of Fear

Prayer: "Jesus, fear or self judgement often feels like that uninvited guest who overstays their welcome. Help me recognize when my inner critic or negativity is holding me back. I want to step into the life You've designed for me."

Scripture Reference: "Do not fear, for I have redeemed you; I have summoned you by name; you are mine." —Isaiah 43:1

Contemplation: What fears are keeping you stuck in the past?

Daily Reminder: "Courage is not the absence of fear, but the decision to move forward despite it."

Engaging Prompt: Identify one fear you want to confront this month. What's your action plan?

My Tender Prayer: "God, remind me to stay present in my body. Help me cultivate awareness of how I feel physically and emotionally. Amen."

Reflection Prompt: Spend a few minutes focusing on your breath. How does being present in your body affect your mood?

March 11: God, I Want to Appreciate My Journey

Prayer: "Hey God, I often forget to appreciate the journey. In the moment, over the course of a day, a whole week passes by, and now maybe it has been a month since I have called that friend."

Scripture Reference: "Count it all joy, my brothers, when you meet trials of various kinds." —James 1:2

Contemplation: How can you appreciate your journey and the lessons learned?

Daily Reminder: "Every step, even the hard ones, has a purpose."

Engaging Prompt: List three things you appreciate about your journey so far.

My Tender Prayer: "Lord, teach me to enjoy food as a source of nourishment and pleasure. Help me appreciate each meal. Amen."

Reflection Prompt: What is your favorite meal? Describe it in detail and savor the memories associated with it.

March 12: God, I Want to Release Comparison

Prayer: "Jesus, comparison is the thief of joy, and I'm tired of letting it steal my happiness. Help me recognize that each twist and turn has shaped me. I want to celebrate my growth and be grateful for the lessons learned along the way. Help me to focus on my unique path instead of comparing my journey to others. I want to celebrate my individuality and trust Your plan for me."

Scripture Reference: "For we are each responsible for our own conduct." —Galatians 6:5

Contemplation: In what areas of your life do you find yourself comparing?

Daily Reminder: "My journey is mine alone, and it's beautiful."

Engaging Prompt: Reflect on your unique qualities. What do you love about yourself?

My Tender Prayer: "Heavenly Father, may I appreciate my body's resilience. Help me acknowledge all it has overcome. Amen."

Reflection Prompt: Reflect on a time when your body showed resilience. How did that experience change your perspective on your body?

March 13: God, I Want to Seek Healing

Prayer: "Hey God, healing feels like a long road, I know I can't take an express rail, but I want to travel it with You. Help me to seek the healing I need—emotionally, spiritually, and physically. Remind me that it's okay to take the time I need to mend."

Scripture Reference: "He heals the brokenhearted and binds up their wounds." —Psalm 147:3

Contemplation: What area of your life needs healing?

Daily Reminder: "Healing is a journey, not a race."

Engaging Prompt: Call a friend.

My Tender Prayer: "God, help me embrace my sensuality as a natural part of being human. Teach me to honor and celebrate this gift. Amen."

Reflection Prompt: What does sensuality mean to you? How can you embrace it in your life?

March 14: God, I Want to Learn from My Mistakes

Prayer: "Jesus, mistakes are like embarrassing photos— Who took THAT pic?! Why did I wear THAT? I wish I could hide them, but they're part of my story. Help me to learn from my mistakes instead of dwelling on them. I want to use those lessons to grow and move forward."

Scripture Reference: "Wisdom is found in those who take advice." —Proverbs 13:10

Contemplation: What mistakes have taught you valuable lessons?

Daily Reminder: "Mistakes are opportunities for growth."

Engaging Prompt: Write about a mistake you've made and the lesson it taught you. How can you apply this lesson moving forward?

My Tender Prayer: "Dear Lord, may I learn to express my emotions through movement. Help me to dance, stretch, and be free in my body. Amen."

Reflection Prompt: Spend some time dancing or moving freely today. How did it feel to express yourself through your body?

March 15: God, I Want to Break the Cycle of Hurt

Prayer: "Hey God, sometimes we don't even notice the path we are on. I don't want to repeat the same patterns that have hurt me in the past. Help me to identify and break those cycles so I can create healthier relationships moving forward. I want to pave a new path."

Scripture Reference: "Do not be conformed to this world but be transformed by the renewal of your mind." —Romans 12:2

Contemplation: What patterns do you see in your past that you want to change?

Daily Reminder: "Breaking the cycle starts with me."

Engaging Prompt: Identify one pattern or habit you want to break. What new behavior can you practice instead?

My Tender Prayer: "God, help me create a self-care routine that nourishes my body, mind, and spirit. May I prioritize my well-being. Amen."

Reflection Prompt: Outline a self-care routine for the week. What activities will you include to nourish your body?

March 16: God, I Want to Embrace Vulnerability

Prayer: "Jesus, being vulnerable, being open, being earnest can feel scarier than dating in the digital age. Help me to embrace vulnerability as a strength, not a weakness. I want to open my heart to others without fear of getting hurt."

Scripture Reference: "Carry each other's burdens, and in this way, you will fulfill the law of Christ." —Galatians 6:2

Contemplation: What fears do you have about being vulnerable with others?

Daily Reminder: "Vulnerability leads to deeper connections."

Engaging Prompt: Write down one way you can be vulnerable with someone this week. How can this strengthen your relationship?

My Tender Prayer: "Lord, help me appreciate the beauty in imperfection. Teach me to love my body as it is, flaws and all. Amen."

Reflection Prompt: What imperfection do you struggle to accept? Write about how it adds to your individuality.

March 17: God, I Want to Let Go of Anger

Prayer: "Hey God, anger can feel like a wildfire burning brightly, fast, rushing, that spreads quickly and burns everything in its path. Help me to release anger that no longer serves me and find healthier ways to express my emotions. I want to be free from its grip."

Scripture Reference: "Get rid of all bitterness, rage, and anger, brawling and slander, along with every form of malice." —Ephesians 4:31

Contemplation: What unresolved anger are you holding onto?

Daily Reminder: "Releasing anger allows room for healing."

Engaging Prompt: Identify one situation where you've felt anger. What steps can you take to process and release it?

My Tender Prayer: "Heavenly Father, remind me that my worth is not defined by my appearance. Help me see beyond the surface. Amen."

Reflection Prompt: What qualities do you possess that contribute to your worth? List them and reflect on their importance.

March 18: God, I Want to Be Present

Prayer: "Jesus, I have a lot on my plate, so much to do, and so many goals. My mind often wanders to the past or worries about the future. Help me to be present in the moment and appreciate the here and now. I want to live fully in each experience without being haunted by what was or what could be."

Scripture Reference: "Therefore do not worry about tomorrow, for tomorrow will worry about itself." —Matthew 6:34

Contemplation: What distractions pull you away from being present?

Daily Reminder: "Being present allows me to enjoy life to its fullest."

Engaging Prompt: Practice mindfulness today. Spend a few moments focusing on your breath and surroundings. How does this shift your perspective?

My Tender Prayer: "God, help me surround myself with positivity and love. May I seek out those who uplift and inspire me. Amen."

Reflection Prompt: Who in your life supports your body positivity? Write about how they inspire you to love yourself.

March 19: God, I Want to Redefine My Identity

Prayer: "Hey God, I'm ready to redefine my identity beyond my past. I am more than what fuels their gossip. Help me see myself through Your eyes—loved, valuable, and full of potential. I want to embrace my true self without the labels that have held me back."

Scripture Reference: "For we are God's handiwork, created in Christ Jesus to do good works." —Ephesians 2:10

Contemplation: What labels have you placed on yourself that no longer fit?

Daily Reminder: "I am more than my past; I am a work in progress."

Engaging Prompt: Write down three positive affirmations about your identity. How can you embody these affirmations daily?

My Tender Prayer: "Dear Lord, may I recognize the power of touch—both to heal and to connect. Help me be mindful of my body's sensations. Amen."

Reflection Prompt: What does a comforting touch feel like to you? Reflect on a time you felt physically comforted.

March 20: God, I Want to Cultivate Joy

Prayer: "Jesus, in this cynical time, joy can sometimes feel like a something that exists on the outskirts, somewhere else. Help me to cultivate joy in my life, even amidst chaos and challenges. I want to find joy in the small things and embrace it fully."

Scripture Reference: "The joy of the Lord is your strength." —Nehemiah 8:10

Contemplation: What brings you joy?

Daily Reminder: "Joy can be inspired action."

Engaging Prompt: List three things that bring you joy. How can you incorporate more of these into your daily life?

My Tender Prayer: "God, teach me to honor my body with nourishing foods that fuel my spirit. Help me cultivate a healthy relationship with food. Amen."

Reflection Prompt: What foods make you feel good? Write about how you can incorporate them more into your meals.

March 21: God, I Want to Learn to Trust Again

Prayer: "Hey God, trust can be hard, especially after being hurt or hearing rumors. Help me to learn to trust again—I want to be able to trust both myself and others. I want to believe in the goodness of people and the promises You've made."

Scripture Reference: "Trust in the Lord with all your heart and lean not on your own understanding." —Proverbs 3:5

Contemplation: Who do you struggle to trust, and why?

Daily Reminder: "Trust is built, not given."

Engaging Prompt: Think of one person you want to work on trusting. What steps can you take to rebuild that trust?

My Tender Prayer: "Lord, may I appreciate the beauty of my body in all its forms. Help me see the divine grace in my physical being. Amen."

Reflection Prompt: Write about a time you felt proud of your body. What were you doing, and how did it feel?

March 22: God, I Want to Be Open to New Experiences

Prayer: "Jesus, help me to be open to new opportunities that come my way. I want to step outside my comfort zone and discover what You have in store for me."

Scripture Reference: "See, I am doing a new thing! Now it springs up; do you not perceive it?" —Isaiah 43:19

Contemplation: What new experiences have you been hesitant to pursue?

Daily Reminder: "Growth happens outside my comfort zone."

Engaging Prompt: Plan one new experience for this week. How can this expand your horizons?

My Tender Prayer: "Heavenly Father, help me to express gratitude for my body every day. May I recognize its strength and abilities. Amen."

Reflection Prompt: What is one thing you can do today to show gratitude for your body?

March 23: God, I Want to Acknowledge My Feelings

Prayer: "Hey God, don't shake me up, I often bottle up my feelings instead of acknowledging them. Help me to recognize and express my emotions in healthy ways that don't bubble over or explode. I want to honor my feelings without being ruled by them."

Scripture Reference: "Do not be anxious about anything, but in every situation, by prayer and petition, with thanksgiving, present your requests to God. And the peace of God, which transcends all understanding, will guard your hearts and your minds in Christ Jesus." —Philippians 4:6-7

Contemplation: What feelings have you been avoiding?

Daily Reminder: "Acknowledging my feelings is a step toward healing."

Engaging Prompt: Write about how you're feeling today. What do these feelings tell you about your current situation?

My Tender Prayer: "God, help me find balance in my life. Teach me to respect my body's limits and honor my needs. Amen."

Reflection Prompt: What areas of your life feel out of balance? What steps can you take to restore that balance?

March 24: God, I Want to Seek Wisdom

Prayer: "Jesus, wisdom is more valuable than gold, but what kind of wisdom do I need right now? Help me to learn from my experiences and those around me. I want to approach life with a wise heart."

Scripture Reference: "Come to me, all you who are weary and burdened, and I will give you rest. Take my yoke upon you and learn from me, for I am gentle and humble in heart, and you will find rest for your souls. For my yoke is easy and my burden is light" — Matthew 11:28-30

Contemplation: Who in your life embodies wisdom?

Daily Reminder: "Wisdom is gained through experiences, both good and bad."

Engaging Prompt: Identify a situation where you need wisdom. What steps can you take to seek guidance?

My Tender Prayer: "Dear Lord, guide me to treat my body with respect. Help me to prioritize rest, exercise, and self-care. Amen."

Reflection Prompt: What does your body need today? Write about how you can respond to its needs.

March 25: God, I Want to Celebrate My Progress

Prayer: "Hey God, I often focus on what I haven't achieved instead of celebrating my progress. This has caused me to overlook amazing experiences in the process of working towards a goal. Help me to acknowledge how far I've come and the steps I've taken toward healing and growth."

Scripture Reference: "Do not despise these small beginnings, for the Lord rejoices to see the work begin." —Zechariah 4:10

Contemplation: What progress have you made recently that deserves recognition?

Daily Reminder: "Every step forward is worth celebrating."

Engaging Prompt: Reflect on three accomplishments, no matter how small, from the past month. How can you celebrate them?

My Tender Prayer: "God, help me to appreciate the journey of self-love. May I celebrate my progress without comparison. Amen."

Reflection Prompt: Trying a new hair style or leaving it messy? Choose your own adventure!

March 26: God, I Want to Let Go of Worry

Prayer: "Jesus, stress and worry often feels like a cloud hovering over me, a rainstorm in fact. Help me to let go of worry about the future and trust that You're in control. I want to live in peace, knowing that I am in Your hands."

Scripture Reference: "Cast all your anxiety on him because he cares for you." —1 Peter 5:7

Contemplation: What worries are occupying your mind?

Daily Reminder: "Worrying doesn't change the outcome; trusting does."

Engaging Prompt: Write down your biggest worry and release it by giving it to God. What can you do to focus on the present instead?

My Tender Prayer: "Lord, may I recognize the persistence of my thoughts. Help me to replace negative self-talk with affirmations of love. Amen."

Reflection Prompt: Time to talk with a friend?

March 27: God, I Want to Rediscover My Passions

Prayer: "Hey God, sometimes life gets busy, and I forget what I'm passionate about in the hustle and grind. Help me to rediscover my passions, instead of chasing an achievement and make time for what really lights me up. I want to embrace my creativity and joy."

Scripture Reference: "Delight yourself in the Lord, and he will give you the desires of your heart." —Psalm 37:4

Contemplation: What activities bring you joy and ignite your passion?

Daily Reminder: "Passion fuels my purpose."

Engaging Prompt: List three passions you want to explore this month. How can you incorporate them into your life?

My Tender Prayer: "Heavenly Father, May I be inspired by the beauty of nature. Help me to connect with my body through the natural world. Amen."

Reflection Prompt: Spend time in nature today. What did you observe, and how did it make you feel about your body?

March 28: God, I Want to Honor My Journey

Prayer: "Jesus, my journey is unique, and I want to honor it. Help me appreciate the twists and turns, knowing that each step has a purpose. I want to embrace my story and recognize its beauty."

Scripture Reference: "For I know the plans I have for you," declares the Lord. —Jeremiah 29:11

Contemplation: How can you honor your journey today?

Daily Reminder: "My story is valuable and worth sharing."

Engaging Prompt: Create a Self-Portrait - Illustrate yourself surrounded by words that describe your strengths and values.

My Tender Prayer: "God, help me to see the beauty in aging. May I embrace the wisdom that comes with each year. Amen."

Reflection Prompt: What do you appreciate about growing older?

March 29: God, I Want to Trust My faith

Prayer: "Hey God, trusting my faith can sometimes feel like trusting a GPS that keeps redirecting and rerouting. Help me to listen to my gut feelings and know when to follow them. I want to learn to trust and embrace the guidance You've placed within me."

Scripture Reference: "Trust in the Lord with all your heart and lean not on your own understanding." —Proverbs 3:5

Contemplation: When have you ignored your faith, and what were the results?

Daily Reminder: "My faith is a gift from You, guiding me toward what's best."

Engaging Prompt: Think of a situation where you should have trusted your gut. How can you practice listening to your faith moving forward?

My Tender Prayer: "Dear Lord, may I cultivate a loving relationship with my body. Help me to appreciate it as a sacred vessel. Amen."

Reflection Prompt: What actions can you take this week to strengthen your relationship with your body?

March 30: God, I Want to Focus on the Future

Prayer: "Jesus, knowing what to do now in order to plan for the future can feel overwhelming, but I want to focus on the possibilities ahead. Help me to let go of my past and look forward with hope and excitement. I trust that You have amazing plans for me."

Scripture Reference: "For I know the plans I have for you," declares the Lord. "Plans to prosper you and not to harm you, plans to give you hope and a future." —Jeremiah 29:11

Contemplation: What hopes do you have for your future?

Daily Reminder: "The future is bright when I walk in faith."

Engaging Prompt: Write down three goals or dreams for the future. What steps can you take to start pursuing them?

My Tender Prayer: "God, thank You for the gift of life and the body I inhabit. Help me to celebrate each day with love and gratitude. Amen."

Reflection Prompt: Collage of Confidence- Get crafty, cut out images and words from magazines that symbolize self-love and empowerment artfully.

March 31: God, I Want to Reflect on My Growth

Prayer: "Hey God, as the month comes to a close, I want to take a moment to reflect on my growth. Help me to see how I've changed and what I've learned. I want to celebrate my journey and the steps I've taken toward healing."

Scripture Reference: "Therefore, if anyone is in Christ, the new creation has come: The old has gone, the new is here!" —2 Corinthians 5:17

Contemplation: How have you grown this month?

Daily Reminder: "Reflection is the first step to transformation."

Engaging Prompt: Review your journal entries from this month. What themes stand out? How have you changed, and what will you carry into the next month?

My Tender Prayer: "Lord, as this month comes to an end, may I carry the lessons of self-love and body positivity with me into the next. Amen."

Reflection Prompt: Heart Map- Create a visual map of your heart, detailing the people, experiences, and places that have shaped you.

Seasonal Message for April, May, and June

Welcome to the next leg of your journey! As we step into April, May, and June, we're diving even deeper into the complexities of our hearts and souls. Life isn't just about the highs; it's also about the lessons learned in the lows. These months invite you to explore forgiveness, ambition, and the beautiful uniqueness that makes you who you are.

April: Forgiveness & Grace

Ah, April—a month of renewal, blooming flowers, and the sweet release that comes from forgiveness. Forgiveness isn't just about saying, "I'm sorry" or "I forgive you." It's a process, a journey that often feels like a rollercoaster ride of emotions. In this month, we'll confront the past and find the grace to let it go. Whether it's forgiving yourself for past mistakes or extending grace to others, we'll explore the transformative power of forgiveness. This isn't about ignoring the hurt; it's about healing and stepping into the freedom that grace offers.

May: Ambition, Dreams, & Hustle

As spring unfolds into full bloom, May brings with it a wave of ambition and dreams. This is your month to dream big and enjoy life! God has placed unique gifts and desires within you, and it's time to embrace them fully. Whether you're eyeing a new career path, planning a passion project, or simply trying to figure out what lights your fire, this month is all about igniting your potential. Together, we'll tackle the fears that hold us back and replace them with the determination to chase our dreams fearlessly. Let's get after it!

June: Overcoming Insecurities & Embracing Our Unique Place in the World

As we welcome June, it's time to kick those insecurities to the curb! In a world that often pushes us to conform, it's essential to recognize and celebrate our unique place. You are not just another face in the crowd; you are a one-of-a-kind masterpiece created by God. This month, we'll dig into the roots of our insecurities and learn how to embrace our individuality. By leaning into our authentic selves, we'll find the confidence to shine in a world that desperately needs our light. Get ready to step into your power!

April: Forgiveness & Grace

True forgiveness is like a winding road through emotions that requires patience and courage. This month, we'll confront old wounds and lean into the grace needed to release them. Whether it's forgiving yourself for past missteps or extending grace to others, we'll uncover the freedom that comes with letting go. Forgiveness isn't about dismissing the hurt—it's about healing through God's love and stepping into the peace that only grace can offer.

April 1: God, Help Me to Forgive Myself

Prayer: "Hey God, teach me that my worth isn't defined by my missteps or how others have treated me."

Scripture Reference: "If we confess our sins, he is faithful and just and will forgive us our sins and purify us from all unrighteousness." —1 John 1:9

Contemplation: What past mistakes are you holding onto that you need to release?

Daily Reminder: "Forgiveness is the key to my freedom."

Engaging Prompt: Write a letter to yourself expressing forgiveness.

My Tender Prayer "Dear God, help me embrace all my emotions—the joyful and the painful. Teach me to see them as sacred expressions of who I am. Amen."
Reflection Prompt: What would you say to someone else in your shoes?

April 2: God, Help Me to Extend Grace to Others

Prayer: "Jesus, I know I'm not perfect, but with choreographed updates, and face tune, sometimes it's hard to remember that others aren't either. Help me to extend grace and understanding to those around me, especially when they mess up."

Scripture Reference: "Be kind and compassionate to one another, forgiving each other, just as in Christ God forgave you." —Ephesians 4:32

Contemplation: Who in your life could use a little more grace right now?

Daily Reminder: "Grace is the gift I give and receive."

Engaging Prompt: Think of someone you need to forgive. Write down three things they've taught you, even though the hurt.

My Tender Prayer: "Lord, allow me to experience life fully through my senses. Let me savor each moment, touch, taste, and smell with gratitude. Amen."

Reflection Prompt: Engage one sense intentionally today—whether it's touch, smell, or sound. Describe the experience and how it made you feel more connected to yourself.

April 3: God, I Want to Release Bitterness

Prayer: "Hey God, I think I know holding onto bitterness is like drinking poison and expecting someone else to suffer. Yet, there are some things I keep looking back at. Help me to release the bitterness that's taking up space in my heart and replace it with your love."

Scripture Reference: "Get rid of all bitterness, rage and anger, brawling and slander, along with every form of malice." —Ephesians 4:31

Contemplation: What bitterness are you holding onto that's keeping you from peace?

Daily Reminder: "Bitterness has no place in my heart."

Engaging Prompt: Write down the source of your bitterness. How can you let it go today?

My Tender Prayer: "God, teach me to honor my feelings as valid and important. Help me create a safe space to express them openly. Amen."

Reflection Prompt: What feelings do you often hide? Write about a safe space where you can express these emotions.

April 4: God, Teach Me the Power of Apology

Prayer: "Jesus, I want to be someone who owns my mistakes and seeks to make things right. But also, is gentle with myself. Help me to understand the power of a sincere apology and to offer it when necessary."

Scripture Reference: "First go and be reconciled to them; then come and offer your gift." —Matthew 5:23-24

Contemplation: When was the last time you apologized? How did it feel?

Daily Reminder: "An apology is a step toward healing."

Engaging Prompt: Think of someone you owe an apology. Write out what you want to say and how you plan to approach them.

My Tender Prayer: "Dear Lord, may I find joy in the full range of my emotions. Help me to appreciate how they guide me on my journey. Amen."

Reflection Prompt: Choose one emotion you often overlook. Reflect on how it has played a role in your life.

April 5: God, I Want to Be a Forgiving Person

Prayer: "Hey God, I want to be known as someone who light-heartedly forgives easily. Help me to release grudges and create a heart that reflects your love and mercy."

Scripture Reference: "For if you forgive other people when they sin against you, your heavenly Father will also forgive you." —Matthew 6:14

Contemplation: How can you embody forgiveness in your daily life?

Daily Reminder: "Forgiveness is a strength, not a weakness."

Engaging Prompt: List three people you find it hard to forgive. What steps can you take to soften your heart toward them?

My Tender Prayer: "God, help me to be vulnerable with those who deserve my trust. Teach me that sharing my feelings can deepen my connections. Amen."

Reflection Prompt: Who do you feel safe sharing your emotions with? Write about a time you opened to them and how it felt.

April 6: God, Help Me to See My Worth

Prayer: "Jesus, I often let my past define me, but I want to see myself through your eyes. Help me to understand that my worth is not based on the past or my mistakes but on Your unconditional love."

Scripture Reference: "You are precious and honored in my sight, and I love you." —Isaiah 43:4

Contemplation: What lies have you believed about your worth? Or ability to pivot?

Daily Reminder: "I am worthy of love and grace."

Engaging Prompt: Write down three things you love about yourself that have nothing to do with your past.

My Tender Prayer: "Lord, guide me to embrace my sensuality as a beautiful part of my being. Help me honor my desires without shame. Amen."

Reflection Prompt: What does sensuality mean to you? Explore this concept in writing or through artistic expression.

April 7: God, Help Me to Accept Your Grace

Prayer: "Hey God, sometimes it's hard to accept the grace you offer, or recognize the chance to delight in the daily activities. Help me to understand that I don't have to earn your love; it's already mine, no matter my past."

Scripture Reference: "But he said to me, 'My grace is sufficient for you, for my power is made perfect in weakness.'" —2 Corinthians 12:9

Contemplation: How can you embrace God's grace in your life today?

Daily Reminder: "God's grace is enough for me."

Engaging Prompt: Reflect on a time when you felt unworthy. How did God's grace show up in that situation?

My Tender Prayer: "Heavenly Father, help me understand the connection between my emotions and my body. Teach me to listen to what they reveal. Amen."

Reflection Prompt: How do you physically feel when you experience strong emotions? Journal about these connections.

April 8: God, I Want to Let Go of Regret

Prayer: "Jesus, I regret silly things, dumb things, even things that don't really matter. Yet, regret can be a heavy burden regardless. Help me to let go of what I can't change and to focus on the lessons learned. I want to move forward with hope."

Scripture Reference: "Forget the former things; do not dwell on the past. See, I am doing a new thing!" —Isaiah 43:18-19

Contemplation: What regrets have you been holding onto?

Daily Reminder: "Regret is not my home; it's a steppingstone."

Engaging Prompt: Write down a regret and the lesson it taught you. How can you use that lesson to grow?

My Tender Prayer: "God, may I learn to express my feelings through creative outlets. Help me to channel my emotions into art, music, or dance. Amen."

Reflection Prompt: What creative outlet resonates with you? Dedicate time to express yourself through this medium today.

April 9: God, Help Me to Embrace Vulnerability

Prayer: "Hey God, not really know what my next steps will be, living in that vulnerability can be scary, but I know it's necessary for growth. Help me to be open and honest about my feelings, both with myself and others."

Scripture Reference: "Confess your sins to each other and pray for each other so that you may be healed." —James 5:16

Contemplation: What keeps you from being vulnerable with others?

Daily Reminder: "Vulnerability is strength, not weakness."

Engaging Prompt: Think of someone you trust. Share a feeling or experience with them that you've been holding onto.

My Tender Prayer: "Dear Lord, remind me that it's okay to feel deeply. Help me to appreciate the beauty of my emotional depth. Amen."

Reflection Prompt: Write about a time when your emotions felt overwhelming. What did you learn about yourself from that experience?

April 10: God, I Want to Be a Light of Grace

Prayer: "Jesus, help me to be a source of happiness, grace and motivation in the lives of others. I want to spread your love and compassion, reminding those around me that they are worthy of love and forgiveness, too."

Scripture Reference: "In the same way, let your light shine before others, that they may see your good deeds and glorify your Father in heaven." —Matthew 5:16

Contemplation: How can you be a light of grace to someone this week?

Daily Reminder: "My light shines brightest when I share grace."

Engaging Prompt: Identify one way you can show kindness or grace to someone today.

My Tender Prayer: "God, help me to release any shame I carry around my desires. Teach me to embrace my sensuality as a divine gift. Amen."

Reflection Prompt: What desires do you feel ashamed of? Write a letter to yourself, affirming that it's okay to want what you want.

April 11: God, Help Me to Heal from Past Hurts

Prayer: "Hey God, let's be honest, the past is complicated. Help me to walk through this process with you by my side."

Scripture Reference: "He heals the brokenhearted and binds up their wounds." —Psalm 147:3

Contemplation: What past hurts do you need to address for healing to begin?

Daily Reminder: "Healing is a journey, not a destination."

Engaging Prompt: Write about a hurt you want to heal. How can you take a step toward healing today?

My Tender Prayer: "Lord, guide me to create habits that honor my emotions and sensuality. Help me make space for these sacred practices. Amen."

Reflection Prompt: What habits can you create to celebrate your emotions?

April 12: God, I Want to Celebrate My Growth

Prayer: "Jesus, sometimes I forget to celebrate my progress. Help me to recognize how far I've come and to honor my growth with gratitude."

Scripture Reference: "Give thanks in all circumstances; for this is the will of God in Christ Jesus for you." —1 Thessalonians 5:18

Contemplation: Where do you feel at ease that you hadn't previously?

Daily Reminder: "Celebrating my growth is part of my journey."

Engaging Prompt: Make a list of milestones you're proud of. How can you celebrate these achievements?

My Tender Prayer: "Heavenly Father, May I find strength in loving my body. Help me to embrace openness as a source of connection and healing. Amen."

Reflection Prompt: Draw a whimsical representation of a memorable relationship or experience that taught you a lesson.

April 13: God, Teach Me to Trust Your Timing

Prayer: "Hey God, I have denied myself the joy you have promised. Help me reconnect with those values."

Scripture Reference: "He has made everything beautiful in its time." —Ecclesiastes 3:11

Contemplation: How have you seen God's timing play out in your life?

Daily Reminder: "Trusting God's timing brings peace."

My Tender Prayer: "God, teach me to use my senses to connect with my emotions. Help me find joy in the little moments of life. Amen."

Reflection Prompt: Take a moment to savor your favorite food or drink. How did engaging your senses enhance your experience?

April 14: God, Help Me to Seek Reconciliation

Prayer: "Jesus, I know reconciliation isn't always easy, and honestly, it can feel overwhelming at times. But I also know it might be worth it. Help me find the courage to soften my heart and take the first step toward mending the relationships that matter. Guide me to speak with grace and listen with love. Teach me how to build bridges where there are walls."

Scripture Reference: "If it is possible, as far as it depends on you, live at peace with everyone." —Romans 12:18

Contemplation: Who in your life needs reconciliation?

Daily Reminder: "Reconciliation is a gift I give myself and others."

Engaging Prompt: Consider writing a note or reaching out to someone you want to reconnect with.

My Tender Prayer: "Dear Lord, may I be patient with myself as I navigate my emotions. Help me to allow my feelings to unfold naturally. Amen."

Reflection Prompt: What emotions do you often rush to suppress? Write about the importance of allowing them to be present.

April 15: God, I Want to Be Gentle with Myself

Prayer: "Hey God, I can be my own worst critic. Help me to practice gentleness with myself, especially when I stumble."

Scripture Reference: "A bruised reed he will not break, and a smoldering wick he will not snuff out." —Isaiah 42:3

Contemplation: What harsh words do you say to yourself that need to be replaced with kindness?

Daily Reminder: "Gentleness is a strength that nurtures my spirit."

Engaging Prompt: Write a list of gentle reminders to yourself for those tough days ahead.

My Tender Prayer: "God, guide me to cultivate a deeper connection with my body and its sensations. Teach me to honor what it feels. Amen."

Reflection Prompt: What sensations do you enjoy experiencing in your body? Reflect on how you can invite more of these sensations into your life.

April 16: God, Help Me to Practice Gratitude

Prayer: "Jesus, I know gratitude shifts my perspective. Help me to focus on the blessings in my life, even amid the struggles of the everyday."

Scripture Reference: "Give thanks to the Lord, for he is good; his love endures forever." —Psalm 136:1

Contemplation: What are three things you're grateful for today?

Daily Reminder: "Gratitude opens my heart to joy."

Engaging Prompt: Start a gratitude list. Write down at least five things you appreciate today.

My Tender Prayer: "Lord, help me to be gentle with myself during times of emotional struggle. May I treat myself with compassion and care. Amen."

Reflection Prompt: When you're feeling down, what comforts you? Create a self-care toolkit for those tough days.

April 17: God, I Want to Let Go of Perfectionism

Prayer: "Hey God, perfectionism has been a heavy weight for me. Help me to embrace my imperfections and recognize that it's okay to be human."

Scripture Reference: "For we are God's handiwork, created in Christ Jesus to do good works, which God prepared in advance for us to do." —Ephesians 2:10

Contemplation: What perfectionist tendencies do you need to let go of?

Daily Reminder: "Perfection is not my goal; growth is."

Engaging Prompt: List three areas where you can allow yourself to be imperfect.

My Tender Prayer: "Heavenly Father, may I see my emotions as teachers. Help me learn from each experience, joyful or painful. Amen."

Reflection Prompt: What lesson have you learned from a difficult emotion? Write about how it has shaped you.

April 18: God, Help Me to Seek Your Will

Prayer: "Jesus, I want to align my desires with my best interests. Help me to seek your guidance in all I do and to trust in your plans for my life."

Scripture Reference: "Trust in the Lord with all your heart and lean not on your own understanding." —Proverbs 3:5

Contemplation: What areas of your life do you need to seek God's will?

Daily Reminder: "God's will for me is greater than my own."

Engaging Prompt: Spend time in prayer, asking God to reveal his will for you in this season of your life.

My Tender Prayer: "God, allow me to express my desires with confidence. Teach me that it's okay to want pleasure and joy in my life. Amen."

Reflection Prompt: Joyful Moments- Paint or draw a scene from a joyful memory. What feelings does it evoke?

April 19: God, I Want to Embrace Change

Prayer: "Lord, guide me to plant seeds of greatness today. Show me the way forward, even if I can't see the whole path yet."

Scripture Reference: "Therefore, if anyone is in Christ, the new creation has come: The old has gone, the new is here!" —2 Corinthians 5:17

Contemplation: What action will you take today toward your biggest goal?

Daily Reminder: "Change is an opportunity for growth."

Engaging Prompt: List three changes you're currently facing. How can you approach them with an open heart?

My Tender Prayer: "Dear Lord, help me find ways to celebrate my body's sensuality. Teach me to honor my desires in healthy ways. Amen."

Reflection Prompt: What are some ways you can celebrate your sensuality this week? Plan at least one activity.

April 20: God, I Want to Cultivate Joy

Prayer: "Hey Jesus, I get it—joy isn't just about feeling good all the time. It's a vibe, a choice, and honestly, a little magic from connecting with the world and the people around me. Help me find those moments of joy in the everyday stuff—in the sunshine on my face, a laugh with a friend, or even just a really good cup of coffee. Show me how to keep that joy alive, even when life feels messy. Teach me to choose it, chase it, and spread it, no matter what challenges come my way."

Scripture Reference: "The joy of the Lord is my strength." —Nehemiah 8:10

Contemplation: What brings you joy?

Daily Reminder: "Joy is my strength, regardless of my circumstances."

Engaging Prompt: Write down three things that bring you joy and commit to incorporating them into your week.

My Tender Prayer: "God, May I release any judgments I hold against myself regarding my emotions. Teach me to accept them with grace. Amen."

Reflection Prompt: What fuels your ambition?

April 21: God, I Want to Be a Peacemaker

Prayer: "Hey God, I want to be a soothing force, in a world that often promotes division. Help me to bring peace into my relationships and communities."

Scripture Reference: "Let us therefore make every effort to do what leads to peace and to mutual edification." —Romans 14:19

Contemplation: How can you be a peacemaker in your life today?

Daily Reminder: "Creating peace starts with me."

Engaging Prompt: Think of a conflict you can help resolve. What steps can you take to bring peace?

My Tender Prayer: "Lord, help me explore the connection between my body and my feelings. May I honor the messages my body conveys. Amen."

Reflection Prompt: When do you feel most empowered?

April 22: God, Help Me to Let Go of Control

Prayer: "God, help me see myself through your eyes—powerful, beautiful, and worthy."

Scripture Reference: "Cast all your anxiety on him because he cares for you." —1 Peter 5:7

Contemplation: I am made for freedom.

Daily Reminder: Show up as my full self, no matter what.

Engaging Prompt: Write down a situation you're trying to control. How can you surrender it to God?

My Tender Prayer: "Heavenly Father, may I celebrate my body's capacity for pleasure. Help me to seek joy in every moment. Amen."

Reflection Prompt: "Prayers for the Bold, Beautiful, and Unapologetically Imperfect"

April 23: God, I Want to Live in the Present

Prayer: "Hey God, you know we humans are a hot mess sometimes—always stressing about what's next or obsessing over what went wrong. Help me hit pause on all that noise and just *be* here, right now, in this moment. Teach me how to soak up the good stuff, laugh a little louder, and maybe even chill out when things don't go as planned. Remind me that life's happening *right now,* and I don't want to miss it. Amen."

Scripture Reference: "Therefore do not worry about tomorrow, for tomorrow will worry about itself." —Matthew 6:34

Contemplation: How can you practice mindfulness in your daily life?

Daily Reminder: Embrace both your flaws and flair.

Engaging Prompt: Take a moment to observe your surroundings right now. Write down what you see, hear, and feel.

My Tender Prayer: "God, teach me to appreciate the ebb and flow of my emotions. Help me understand that it's natural to experience highs and lows. Amen."

Reflection Prompt: Go thrift shopping for a wildly artistic outfit.

April 24: God, Help Me to Trust in Your Plan

Prayer: "Father, remind me that I don't need to fit in. I was born to stand out."

Scripture Reference: "The Lord does not look at the things people look at. People look at the outward appearance, but the Lord looks at the heart." —1 Samuel 16:7

Contemplation: What fears keep you from trusting God's plan?

Daily Reminder: "God's plan for me is good, even when I can't see it."

Engaging Prompt: Write down your hopes for the future. Pray over them, asking God to align your dreams with His plans.

My Tender Prayer: "Dear Lord, may I embrace my emotional landscape. Teach me to express my feelings with honesty and integrity. Amen."

Reflection Prompt: What feelings do you often hide from others? How can you begin to share them in a safe way?

April 25: God, Help Me to Honor My Journey

Prayer: "Hey God, Whether I'm wearing something trendy or creating my own style, I often compare myself to others and forget my unique journey. Help me to honor my path and the lessons I've learned along the way."

Scripture Reference: "We all have different gifts, according to the grace given to each of us." —Romans 12:6

Contemplation: How can you celebrate your unique journey?

Daily Reminder: "My journey is mine alone, and it is beautiful."

Engaging Prompt: Draw an outfit that represents your style if nothing constricted your expression.

My Tender Prayer: "God, help me find beauty in my laughter. Amen."

Reflection Prompt: What part of your authentic self are you embracing?

April 26: God, I Want to Embrace My Story

Prayer: "Jesus, my life's been a whole rollercoaster—twists, turns, and some wild drops—but it's *my* story, and I'm owning it. Help me to embrace every high and low, every win and oops, because it's all part of what makes me *me*. Show me how to see the beauty in the chaos and the lessons in the hard stuff. Thank You for providing for me every step of the way, even when I didn't see it. Let me wear my journey with a smile, knowing You've been with me through it all. Amen."

Scripture Reference: "And we know that in all things God works for the good of those who love him, who have been called according to his purpose." —Romans 8:28

Contemplation: What part of your story are you struggling to embrace?

Daily Reminder: "My story is valuable and worthy of being told."

Engaging Prompt: Write about a defining moment in your life. How has it shaped who you are today?

My Tender Prayer: "Lord, guide me to practice emotional self-care. Help me to prioritize my mental and emotional well-being. Amen."

Reflection Prompt: What makes you feel safe?

April 27: God, Help Me to Practice Self-Care

Prayer: "Hey God, I know I've got this habit of putting everyone else first and running myself ragged in the process. Help me hit the brakes and remember that taking care of *me* isn't selfish—it's how I honor the amazing person You created. Teach me to see self-care as part of Your plan, not some guilty indulgence. Show me how to rest, recharge, and love myself the way You love me. And maybe remind me now and then that I can't pour from an empty cup."

Scripture Reference: "Love your neighbor as yourself." —Mark 12:31

Contemplation: What self-care practices do you need to incorporate into your life?

Daily Reminder: "Self-care is not selfish; it's essential."

Engaging Prompt: Create a self-care plan for the week. What will you do to nurture yourself?

My Tender Prayer: "Heavenly Father, may I find comfort in my emotions, knowing they are valid and important. Help me to feel without fear. Amen."

Reflection Prompt: Do I have the courage to own my voice unapologetically?

April 28: God, I Want to Make Amends

Prayer: "Jesus, I know that sometimes I hurt others without realizing it. Careless and clumsy, help me to seek amends where I can and to take responsibility for my actions."

Scripture Reference: "Bear with each other and forgive one another if any of you has a grievance against someone. Forgive as the Lord forgave you." —Colossians 3:13

Contemplation: Is there someone you need to make amends with?

Daily Reminder: "Taking responsibility is a step toward healing."

Engaging Prompt: List any relationships you need to mend. What steps will you take to reach out?

My Tender Prayer: "God, help me to appreciate the role of my emotions in my life. Teach me to see them as part of my divine journey. Amen."

Reflection Prompt: Reflect on a time when your emotions guided you toward a decision. What did you learn from that experience?

April 29: God, I Want to Learn to Let Go

Prayer: "Hey God, I struggle with holding on to things that no longer serve me. Sometimes out of loyalty, nostalgia or reasons I do not understand. Help me to learn the art of letting go and trusting you with what's next."

Scripture Reference: "Let us hold unswervingly to the hope we profess, for he who promised is faithful." —Hebrews 10:23

Contemplation: What are you holding onto that you need to release?

Daily Reminder: "Letting go creates space for new beginnings."

Engaging Prompt: Write a letter to something or someone you need to let go of. Afterward, consider safely burning or discarding it as a symbolic gesture.

My Tender Prayer: "Dear Lord, guide me to seek joy and pleasure in my daily life. Help me cultivate gratitude for these moments. Amen."

Reflection Prompt: What small pleasures bring you joy? Write about how you can incorporate more of these into your routine.

April 30: God, Help Me to Be Mindful of My Words

Prayer: "Jesus, my words hold power. Help me to be mindful of what I say, ensuring my words uplift and encourage rather than tear down."

Scripture Reference: "The tongue has the power of life and death, and those who love it will eat its fruit." —Proverbs 18:21

Contemplation: How can you use your words to promote forgiveness and grace?

Daily Reminder: "My words can build up or tear down; I choose to build up."

Engaging Prompt: Think of someone you can encourage with your words today. Write them a note or send them a message.

My Tender Prayer: "God, help me embrace my gifts as a woman. Amen."

Reflection Prompt: Your pleasure is important.

May: Ambition, Dreams, & Hustle

As spring blossoms in full, May stirs a fresh wave of ambition and purpose. This is your time to dream boldly and step into the hustle with faith and fire! God has planted unique talents and desires in your heart, and now is the moment to nurture them. Whether you're pursuing a new career, launching a passion project, or still discovering what sparks your soul, this month is about embracing your God-given potential. Together, we'll confront the fears holding us back and replace them with courage and determination. It's time to show up, shine bright, and chase those dreams with everything you've got!

May 1: God, Ignite My Ambition

Prayer: "Hey God, I have a lot of interests, but I don't know what to focus on. I feel that spark of ambition within me. Light that fire so I can pursue my dreams with passion and purpose."

Scripture Reference: "Delight yourself in the Lord, and he will give you the desires of your heart." —Psalm 37:4

Contemplation: What dreams are you excited to chase this month?

Daily Reminder: "My ambition is a gift from God, and I will use it wisely."

My Tender Prayer: "God, teach me to embrace the freedom of moving forward. Amen."
Reflection Prompt: Dancing in the Rain- Reflect on a moment when you let loose, danced freely, and felt God's joy washing over you.
Engaging Prompt: List three dreams you want to pursue this month. What steps can you take to get started?

May 2: God, Help Me to Take Risks

Prayer: "Jesus, I know that growth often comes from stepping outside my comfort zone. Help me to embrace risks for the sake of my dreams."

Scripture Reference: "Fear not, for I have redeemed you; I have called you by name, you are mine." —Isaiah 43:1

Contemplation: What risk do you feel called to take right now?

Daily Reminder: "Taking risks is part of my journey toward success."

Engaging Prompt: Write down a fear holding you back. What's one small step you can take to overcome it?

My Tender Prayer: "Lord, give me the courage to take risks creatively. Make space in my heart for love and peace so I can also prosper. Amen."

Reflection Prompt: Moments of Courage- Describe a time you took a leap of faith in your life, love, or career, and what you learned from it.

May 3: God, Help Me Stay Focused

Prayer: "Hey God, distractions are everywhere! Help me to stay focused on my goals and not get sidetracked by empty flattery."

Scripture Reference: "Set your minds on things that are above, not on things that are on earth." —Colossians 3:2

Contemplation: What distractions do you need to eliminate this month?

Daily Reminder: "Focus brings clarity, and clarity brings success."

Engaging Prompt: Create a plan to minimize distractions. What tools or techniques will you use?

My Tender Prayer: "Dear God, help me understand that forgiveness is a gift I give to myself. Teach me to see the beauty in letting go. Amen."

Reflection Prompt: Reflect on a situation where you struggled to believe in yourself. What held you back, and how can you begin to move forward?

May 4: God, Give Me Strength to Hustle

Prayer: "Jesus, some days the hustle feels like learning to master all the skills, leaving little time for your craft. Give me the strength to push through and keep working toward my dreams."

Scripture Reference: "I can do all this through him who gives me strength." —Philippians 4:13

Contemplation: What motivates you to keep hustling, even when it's tough?

Daily Reminder: "Strength comes from within, and I can tap into it."

Engaging Prompt: Identify a quote that inspires you. Write it down and place it where you can see it daily.

My Tender Prayer: "God, may I release the need for others to understand my ambition. Teach me that my peace is worth the sacrifice. Amen."

Reflection Prompt: Treasure Map- Draw a treasure map that symbolizes the journey to self-discovery and fulfillment.

May 5: God, Help Me Celebrate Small Wins

Prayer: "Hey God, I often overlook my progress. Help me to celebrate the small wins that lead to my bigger goals."

Scripture Reference: "Do not despise these small beginnings, for the Lord rejoices to see the work begin." —Zechariah 4:10

Contemplation: What small victories have you achieved lately?

Daily Reminder: "Every step forward, no matter how small, is worth celebrating."

Engaging Prompt: List three small wins from the past week and plan a way to celebrate them!

My Tender Prayer: "Lord, help me let go of the weight of resentment. May I choose to carry love and understanding instead. Amen."

Reflection Prompt: Fierce Woman- Create an image of a fierce woman who embodies strength and resilience. What qualities does she have?

May 6: God, Show Me My Unique Path

Prayer: "Jesus, I want to carve out a unique path that reflects who I am. Help me to embrace my individuality as I pursue my dreams."

Scripture Reference: "Each of you should use whatever gift you have received to serve others, as faithful stewards of God's grace in its various forms." —1 Peter 4:10

Contemplation: How does your unique story shape your ambitions?

Daily Reminder: "My uniqueness is my strength."

Engaging Prompt: Write down what makes you unique. How can you incorporate that into your goals?

My Tender Prayer: "Heavenly Father, may I embrace romancing life, by honoring the tender joyfulness of being myself. Amen."

Reflection Prompt: Love Letter to Myself- Create a visual love letter to yourself, make it a craft project, celebrating your worth and achievements.

May 7: God, Help Me to Find Balance

Prayer: "Hey God, I know ambition is important, but so is rest. Help me to find balance in my hustle."

Scripture Reference: "Come to me, all you who are weary and burdened, and I will give you rest." —Matthew 11:28

Contemplation: How can you incorporate rest into your busy schedule?

Daily Reminder: "Balance is key to sustainable success."

Engaging Prompt: Plan a day for self-care this week. What will you do to recharge?

My Tender Prayer: "God, guide me to acknowledge my feelings of hurt without allowing them to define me. Teach me to rise above. Amen."

Reflection Prompt: Draw anything - anything but spend some time doing it.

May 8: God, Help Me to Collaborate

Prayer: "Jesus, I know teamwork makes the dream work—and let's be real, sometimes I need all the help I can get! Help me find those ride-or-die collaborators who share my vision and energy. Teach me how to work together with grace, respect, and maybe a little humor when things get tricky. Remind me that it's okay to lean on others and that we're stronger when we build something amazing *together*."

Scripture Reference: "Let us consider how we may spur one another on toward love and good deeds, not giving up meeting together, as some are in the habit of doing, but encouraging one another." —Hebrews 10:24-25

Contemplation: Who can you collaborate with to achieve your goals?

Daily Reminder: "Collaboration opens doors that are invisible."

Engaging Prompt: Reach out to someone you admire and explore how you can work together.

My Tender Prayer: "Lord, let me see friendship in others easily. Amen."

Reflection Prompt: A compliment can make someone's day.

May 9: God, I Want to Trust the Process

Prayer: "Hey God, I have been working so hard towards my goals, sometimes it's hard to be patient. Help me to trust the process and know that my efforts will bear fruit in due time."

Scripture Reference: "Be still before the Lord and wait patiently for him." —Psalm 37:7

Contemplation: What challenges are testing your patience right now?

Daily Reminder: "Trusting the process brings peace to my hustle."

Engaging Prompt: Write about a time when patience led to a rewarding outcome.

My Tender Prayer: "Dear God, may I learn that forgiveness does not mean condoning behavior but freeing myself from the past. Amen."

Reflection Prompt: What misconceptions about forgiveness do you hold? Write about how you can shift your perspective.

May 10: God, Help Me to Dream Bigger

Prayer: "Jesus, sometimes I limit my dreams. Help me to dream bigger and envision the incredible possibilities you have for my life."

Scripture Reference: "Now to him who is able to do immeasurably more than all we ask or imagine." —Ephesians 3:20

Contemplation: What dreams have you been afraid to pursue?

Daily Reminder: "I am capable of more than I realize."

Engaging Prompt: Write down your wildest dreams and the first step you can take toward one of them.

My Tender Prayer: "God, help me to honor my desires in ways that are fulfilling. Amen."

Reflection Prompt: What mistakes have you made that still weigh on your heart? Draw a flower you'd give yourself.

May 11: God, Help Me to Stay Committed

Prayer: "Hey God, you know me—I'm all about those big goals when the vibe is high, but when the sparkle fades, oof, it's hard to stay on track. Give me that fire-in-my-soul determination to keep pushing, even when it's not fun or flashy anymore. Help me stay focused, steady, and maybe even a little stubborn in chasing the things that matter. Remind me why I started and keep me moving forward, one step at a time."

Scripture Reference: "Let us not become weary in doing good, for at the proper time we will reap a harvest if we do not give up." —Galatians 6:9

Contemplation: What commitments have you made that need renewed focus?

Daily Reminder: "Commitment is the bridge between goals and accomplishment."

Engaging Prompt: Choose one goal to focus on this month and outline your commitment to it.

My Tender Prayer: "Lord, guide me to practice self-compassion as I navigate my journey of forgiveness. Help me to treat myself with kindness. Amen."

Reflection Prompt: What does self-compassion even look like for you? List ways you can be kinder to yourself.

May 12: God, Help Me to Learn from Failure

Prayer: "Jesus, I know failure is part of the journey. Help me to embrace it as a learning experience rather than a setback. Sulking after learning a lesson doesn't help me move forward in life, so I'll try not to be pouty when things don't go exactly as I expected."

Scripture Reference: "For though the righteous fall seven times, they rise again." —Proverbs 24:16

Contemplation: What recent failure has taught you a valuable lesson?

Daily Reminder: "Failure is not the end; it's a step toward success."

Engaging Prompt: Write about a failure and the lesson it taught you.

My Tender Prayer: "Heavenly Father, may I release the belief that holding onto pain protects me. Teach me that love is my true strength. Amen."

Reflection Prompt: A Letter to My Younger Self- Write a letter to your younger self, reflecting on the lessons you wish you had learned sooner.

May 13: God, Help Me to Inspire Others

Prayer: "Hey God, I want my journey to inspire others. Help me to share my story and lift others as I climb."

Scripture Reference: "Let your light shine before others, that they may see your good deeds and glorify your Father in heaven." —Matthew 5:16

Contemplation: How can your story inspire those around you?

Daily Reminder: "Inspiring others fuels my ambition."

Engaging Prompt: Share a piece of your story with someone who could benefit from it.

My Tender Prayer: "God, help me to find closure in situations that feel unresolved. May I trust that You are guiding my path. Amen."

Reflection Prompt: What unresolved issues linger in your life? Reflect on how you can find closure or peace regarding them.

May 14: God, Help Me to Set Healthy Boundaries

Prayer: "Jesus, ambition can sometimes blur my boundaries. Help me to set healthy limits so I can pursue my dreams without sacrificing my well-being or harming my friendships."

Scripture Reference: "Therefore, whether you eat or drink, or whatever you do, do it all for the glory of God." —1 Corinthians 10:31

Contemplation: What boundaries do you need to establish in your life?

Daily Reminder: "Boundaries are not walls; they're protectors of my peace."

Engaging Prompt: Identify one area where you need to set a boundary this week. What will you do to uphold it?

My Tender Prayer: "Lord, may I celebrate the progress I make on my journey to forgiveness, no matter how small. Teach me to appreciate my growth. Amen."

Reflection Prompt: Sing in the shower.

May 15: God, I Want to Pursue My Passions

Prayer: "Hey God, I want to chase the passions you've placed in my heart. Help me to prioritize what truly matters to me."

Scripture Reference: "Whatever you do, work heartily, as for the Lord and not for men." —Colossians 3:23

Contemplation: What passions have you set aside that deserve more attention?

Daily Reminder: "Pursuing my passions is an act of honoring God."

Engaging Prompt: Make a list of passions you want to pursue this month. Pick one to focus on first.

My Tender Prayer: "Dear God, guide me to set boundaries that honor my healing process. Help me protect my heart as I learn to forgive. Amen."

Reflection Prompt: What boundaries do you need to set in order to support your journey? Write about them.

May 16: God, Help Me to Embrace My Journey

Prayer: "Jesus, every step of my journey is a reflection of my growth, my grace, and my unique sensuality. Help me embrace the beauty of where I've been—every twist, every lesson—and honor it as part of my divine unfolding. Teach me to walk with confidence into where I'm going, with gratitude for the woman I'm becoming. May I always remember that each step, no matter how small, is a celebration of my femininity, my strength, and Your love that guides me through it all."

Scripture Reference: "And we know that in all things God works for the good of those who love him." —Romans 8:28

Contemplation: What aspects of your journey are you grateful for today?

Engaging Prompt: Write about a part of your journey that has shaped you and what you learned from it.

My Tender Prayer: "God, teach me to release the past with love and gratitude for the lessons it has taught me. Amen."

Reflection Prompt: Go for a walk.

May 17: God, Help Me to Believe in Myself

Prayer: "Hey God, I often doubt myself. Help me to believe in my abilities and trust that you have equipped me for success. I feel the urge to do so much more than I already have."

Scripture Reference: "Be strong and courageous. Do not be afraid; do not be discouraged, for the Lord your God will be with you wherever you go." —Joshua 1:9

Contemplation: What skills or qualities do you need to recognize in yourself?

Daily Reminder: "I am equipped and capable of achieving my dreams."

Engaging Prompt: List five things you're good at. How can you leverage these strengths this month?

My Tender Prayer: "Lord, help me understand that loving myself is a journey, not a destination. Grant me patience. Amen."

Reflection Prompt: Try to write a lyric to a song - it doesn't even have to make sense.

May 18: God, Help Me to Dream in Color

Prayer: "Jesus, I want to dream big—bold, vivid, and full of color, not stuck in the dull black-and-white. Help me see my life the way You do—brimming with possibility, excitement, and all the vibrancy You've intended for me. Show me how to live out my dreams like they're the wild, beautiful masterpiece they're meant to be. No more playing small, just walking in full technicolor confidence, with You leading the way."

Scripture Reference: "For I know the plans I have for you, declares the Lord." —Jeremiah 29:11

Contemplation: Where does ambition fit in your life?

Daily Reminder: "My dreams are meant to be bold and colorful."

Engaging Prompt: Create a vision board or mood board that captures your dreams. What colors and images inspire you?

My Tender Prayer: "Heavenly Father, may I learn to trust that by letting go, I create space for new blessings in my life. Amen."

Reflection Prompt: What new beginnings are you ready to invite into your life? Write about how letting go can make room for them.

May 19: God, Help Me to Find My Tribe

Prayer: "Hey God, I want to be surrounded by people who lift me up, who get my vibe and share my vision. Help me find my tribe—the ones who inspire, encourage, and remind me of who I am when I forget. Show me the connections that will help me grow and challenge me to be my best. Let me build a circle of love, support, and energy that matches the big dreams You've placed in my heart."

Scripture Reference: "Be devoted to one another in love. Honor one another above yourselves." — Romans 12:10

Contemplation: Who in your life inspires you to be your best self?

Daily Reminder: "Community is vital for my growth."

Engaging Prompt: Reach out to someone who inspires you. Plan a time to connect or collaborate.

My Tender Prayer: "God, help me to release my attachment to outcomes. Teach me to find peace in the present moment. Amen."

Reflection Prompt: What outcomes do you find yourself obsessing over? Reflect on how releasing that desire could bring you peace.

May 20: God, Help Me to Cultivate Patience

Prayer: "Jesus, I'm out here chasing dreams like I'm on a mission, but let's be real—I'm not the most patient person. Help me slow down and trust in Your timing, even when I feel like everything should be happening yesterday. Teach me that the best things come when I'm ready, not when I want them. Give me the grace to wait with faith."

Scripture Reference: "Wait for the Lord; be strong, and let your heart take courage; wait for the Lord!" —Psalm 27:14

Contemplation: What situations are testing your patience right now?

Daily Reminder: "Patience is the key that unlocks my dreams."

Engaging Prompt: Write down a situation where patience led to positive results in your life.

My Tender Prayer: "Lord, guide me to seek reconciliation where possible, while also honoring my own needs and boundaries. Amen."

Reflection Prompt: Are there relationships in your life that need healing? Write about your hopes for these connections.

May 21: God, Help Me to Take Inspired Action

Prayer: "Hey God, I've got all these dreams bubbling up, and I'm ready to go after them, but I don't want to just run wild without Your direction. Help me to move with purpose, knowing each step is guided by You. Give me the wisdom to act with intention, not just hustle for the sake of it. Let my actions be aligned with Your plan, so I'm not just chasing the dream, but chasing it Your way."

Scripture Reference: "The plans of the diligent lead surely to abundance." —Proverbs 21:5

Contemplation: What action steps feel aligned with your vision?

Daily Reminder: "Taking action is a sign of my faith."

Engaging Prompt: Identify one inspired action you can take today and do it!

My Tender Prayer: "Dear God, may I find strength in my connections. Teach me to open my heart, even when it feels difficult. Amen."

Reflection Prompt: Grace in the Mess- Describe a chaotic moment in your life that ended up teaching you about grace and acceptance.

May 22: God, Help Me to Release Self-Doubt

Prayer: "Jesus, self-doubt creeps in and holds me back. Help me to release it and replace it with your truth."

Scripture Reference: "Therefore, there is now no condemnation for those who are in Christ Jesus." —Romans 8:1

Contemplation: What self-doubts are you ready to release and replace with ambition?

Daily Reminder: "I am worthy of my dreams, and self-doubt has no place in my journey."

Engaging Prompt: Write a letter to yourself, addressing your self-doubts and countering them with affirmations of truth.

My Tender Prayer: "God, help me embrace the uncertainty that comes with letting go. Teach me that the unknown can lead to growth. Amen."

Reflection Prompt: What uncertainties are you facing? Write about how you can approach them with an open heart.

May 23: God, Help Me to Believe in Miracles

Prayer: "Hey God, I want to believe in the miracles you can create in my life. Help me to keep my heart open to your possibilities as I move through my daily life. Allow my ambition to find a beneficial outlet"

Scripture Reference: "Jesus looked at them and said, 'With man this is impossible, but with God all things are possible.'" —Matthew 19:26

Contemplation: What miracles are you hoping for?

Daily Reminder: "Believing in miracles opens doors to the extraordinary."

Engaging Prompt: Encourage a friend to pursue a dream.

My Tender Prayer: "Lord, may I find peace in knowing that peace benefits my well-being. Teach me the power of releasing negativity. Amen."

Reflection Prompt: Reflect on how holding onto resentment affects your life. How would a sense of calmness change your experience?

May 24: God, Help Me to Honor My Journey

Prayer: "Jesus, I want to honor my journey and all the wild, beautiful lessons it's taught me. Help me embrace where I am right now, even when I'm tempted to rush ahead or look back. Let me celebrate the growth, the wins, and yes, even the bumps along the way, because they've all made me who I am today. Teach me to appreciate the present and trust that I'm exactly where I need to be."

Scripture Reference: "The Lord makes firm the steps of the one who delights in him; though he may stumble, he will not fall, for the Lord upholds him with his hand." — Psalm 37:23-24

Contemplation: How can you honor your journey, both past and present?

Daily Reminder: "Every step I take is part of my unique story."

Engaging Prompt: Write a letter to your past self, expressing gratitude for the lessons learned.

My Tender Prayer: "Heavenly Father, help me find the courage to face the emotions tied to my past. Teach me to navigate them with grace. Amen."

Reflection Prompt: What emotions arise when you think about your worthiness? Write about how you can process these feelings healthily.

May 25: God, Help Me to Cultivate Gratitude

Prayer: "Hey God, I want to cultivate gratitude for the journey and the people in my life. Help me to see the good in every situation, even when the situation kinda sucks."

Scripture Reference: "Give thanks in all circumstances; for this is the will of God in Christ Jesus for you." —1 Thessalonians 5:18

Contemplation: What do you think?

Daily Reminder: "Gratitude shifts my perspective."

Engaging Prompt: Do something kind for a stranger today.

My Tender Prayer: "God, guide me to surround myself with supportive people who encourage my journey of healing and forgiveness. Amen."

Reflection Prompt: Who are the people that uplift you? Reflect on how their support can aid your healing process.

May 26: God, Help Me to Embrace Change

Prayer: "Jesus, change can be scary, but I know it's often necessary for growth. Help me to embrace the changes in my life with faith."

Scripture Reference: "Jesus Christ is the same yesterday and today and forever." —Hebrews 13:8

Contemplation: What changes are you currently facing that you need to embrace?

Daily Reminder: "Change brings new opportunities."

Engaging Prompt: Write about a change you resisted in the past but ended up being good for you.

My Tender Prayer: "Lord, teach me that forgiveness does not erase the past but allows me to create a new narrative for my future. Amen."

Reflection Prompt: What narrative do you want to create for your future? Write about how forgiveness can help you shape that story.

May 27: God, Help Me to Be Bold

Prayer: "Hey God, I'm ready to be bold and fearless in chasing my dreams. Help me to take those courageous steps without second-guessing, even when the path feels uncertain. Give me the confidence to move forward with purpose, knowing You've got my back. Show me how to step into my power and take action with strength and grace, without hesitation."

Scripture Reference: "Be strong and courageous. Do not be afraid; do not be discouraged, for the Lord your God will be with you wherever you go." —Joshua 1:9

Contemplation: What does it mean to be bold in your life?

Daily Reminder: "Boldness opens doors to new possibilities."

Engaging Prompt: Identify a bold action you've been putting off. Commit to taking it this week!

My Tender Prayer: "Dear God, May I recognize the strength that comes from forgiving or loving myself and others. Teach me to embrace this power. Amen."

Reflection Prompt: How does forgiving or loving others empower you? Write about the strength you find in forgiveness and love.

May 28: God, Help Me to Stay Curious

Prayer: "Jesus, I want to stay curious, always open to learning and growing. Help me embrace every opportunity to explore, to stretch beyond my comfort zone, and to evolve in every part of my life. Whether it's through new experiences, relationships, or challenges, guide me to stay excited about the journey ahead. Let me remain open to the lessons You have for me, so I can continue to grow into the best version of myself."

Scripture Reference: "Let the wise hear and increase in learning, and the one who understands obtain guidance." —Proverbs 1:5

Contemplation: What are you curious about that you want to explore?

Daily Reminder: "Curiosity fuels my growth."

Engaging Prompt: Choose a new skill or topic to explore this month. What resources will you use to learn?

My Tender Prayer: "God, help me to stay grounded in love as I navigate my journey of reawakening. Teach me to let love guide my heart. Amen."

Reflection Prompt: How can love be a guiding principle in your life? Reflect on moments where love led you to forgiveness.

May 29: God, Help Me to Lead with Love

Prayer: "Hey God, I want to lead with love in everything I do. Whether I'm chasing dreams, building something new, or just navigating the day-to-day, help me approach it all with a heart full of compassion. Teach me to infuse kindness into my ambitions and stay grounded in love, no matter how big the goals or how tough the challenges."

Scripture Reference: "Let all that you do be done in love." —1 Corinthians 16:14

Contemplation: How can you lead with love in your goals?

Daily Reminder: "Love is the foundation of all my actions."

Engaging Prompt: Think of a project or goal where you can incorporate love and compassion. Outline how you will do this.

My Tender Prayer: "Lord, thank You for the lessons of forgiveness. May I forgive myself as well, Amen."

Reflection Prompt: When was the last time you watched the sun set or sun rise.

May 30: God, Help Me to Be Open to Change

Prayer: "Jesus, I know life can get a little wild and unpredictable—one moment it's smooth sailing, and the next, everything's flipped upside down. Help me stay open to the changes You bring my way, even when they feel chaotic. Teach me to trust that You're in control, guiding me through the twists and turns with purpose. Give me the strength to adapt, the wisdom to grow, and the peace to know You've got me, no matter what."

Scripture Reference: "Trust in the Lord with all your heart and lean not on your own understanding; in all your ways submit to him, and he will make your paths straight." —Proverbs 3:5-6

Contemplation: What unexpected changes have you experienced that turned out to be blessings?

Daily Reminder: "Openness to change allows me to grow."

Engaging Prompt: Reflect on a recent change in your life. What did you learn from it?

My Tender Prayer: "Heavenly Father, May I always choose love. Amen."

Reflection Prompt: Take a long drive.

May 31: God, Help Me to Celebrate My Journey

Prayer: "Hey God, as we close out this month, help me to celebrate all the progress I've made and the dreams I'm pursuing or about to pursue."

Scripture Reference: "This is the day that the Lord has made; let us rejoice and be glad in it." —Psalm 118:24

Contemplation: What victories—big or small—do you want to celebrate this month?

Daily Reminder: "Celebrating my journey fuels my ambition."

Engaging Prompt: Plan a mini celebration for yourself. What will you do to honor your progress?

My Tender Prayer: "Heavenly Father, thank You for this body I live in. Help me see it as a temple—worthy, sacred, and beautiful. Amen."

Reflection Prompt: List three things you love about your body. If you feel comfortable, sketch or visualize these features with appreciation.

June: Overcoming Insecurities & Embracing Our Unique Place in the World

As we step into June, it's time to say goodbye to insecurities! In a world that often pressures us to fit in, it's vital to embrace the truth: you are a unique masterpiece, fearfully and wonderfully made by God. You weren't meant to blend in—you were made to stand out. This month, we'll uncover the roots of our self-doubt and replace them with confidence rooted in who God says we are. By leaning into our authentic selves, we'll discover the freedom to shine in ways only we can. Get ready to walk boldly in your God-given power!

June 1: God, Help Me to Accept Myself

Prayer: "Jesus, sometimes I struggle to accept myself just as I am. Help me see myself through your eyes."

Scripture Reference: "So God created mankind in his own image, in the image of God he created them; male and female he created them." —Genesis 1:27

Contemplation: What insecurities do you have that are really silly?

Daily Reminder: "I am fearfully and wonderfully made."

Engaging Prompt: Write a letter to yourself, embracing all your unique qualities.

My Tender Prayer: "God, help me celebrate the joy of movement in my body. May I find delight in every step I take. Amen."

Reflection Prompt: What activities bring you joy? Write or draw about a time when movement made you feel alive.

June 2: God, Help Me to Celebrate My Differences

Prayer: "Hey God, I want to embrace what makes me different instead of hiding it. Help me to celebrate my uniqueness."

Scripture Reference: "God has arranged the parts in the body, every one of them, just as he wanted them to be." —1 Corinthians 12:18

Contemplation: How do your differences add to the world around you?

Daily Reminder: "My uniqueness is my superpower."

Engaging Prompt: Make a list of your unique traits and how they positively impact others.

My Tender Prayer: "Lord, may I discover the beauty of self-expression through movement. Teach me to embrace my unique rhythm. Amen."

Reflection Prompt: What forms of movement resonate with you? How can you incorporate them into your life this week?

June 3: God, Help Me to Be Confident in My Skin

Prayer: "Jesus, I want to walk in confidence, no matter my body shape or size. Help me to love my body as it is."

Scripture Reference: "Your beauty should not come from outward adornment... Rather, it should be that of your inner self." —1 Peter 3:3-4

Contemplation: What do you love about your body?

Daily Reminder: "My worth isn't defined by my appearance."

Engaging Prompt: Take a moment to look in the mirror and say three things you love about yourself.

My Tender Prayer: "Heavenly Father, let me find freedom in dancing—whether in the privacy of my home or among friends. Amen."

Reflection Prompt: When was the last time you danced? Describe the experience and how it made you feel.

June 4: God, Help Me to Silence My Inner Critic

Prayer: "Hey God, my inner critic can be loud and harsh. Help me to silence it and replace those thoughts with your truth."

Scripture Reference: "We demolish arguments and every pretension that sets itself up against the knowledge of God." —2 Corinthians 10:5

Contemplation: What negative self-talk do you need to combat today?

Daily Reminder: "I am enough, just as I am."

Engaging Prompt: Write down a negative thought you often have and counter it with a positive affirmation.

My Tender Prayer: "God, guide me to listen to my body's needs as I move. Help me nurture it with love and respect. Amen."

Reflection Prompt. What does your body need today? Write about how you can honor its requests through movement.

June 5: God, Help Me to Set Healthy Boundaries

Prayer: "Jesus, help me to set boundaries that honor my needs and protect my peace. I want to prioritize my well-being."

Scripture Reference: "Therefore, do not worry about tomorrow, for tomorrow will worry about itself. Each day has enough trouble of its own." —Matthew 6:34

Contemplation: What boundaries do you need to establish in your relationships?

Daily Reminder: "Setting boundaries is an act of self-love."

Engaging Prompt: List three boundaries you want to set this month and how you'll communicate them.

My Tender Prayer: "Lord, help me explore the joy of movement in nature. May I find peace and happiness in the world around me. Amen."

Reflection Prompt: Spend time outdoors today. Write about how nature makes you feel and the joy you find in movement there.

June 6: God, Help Me to Let Go of Comparison

Prayer: "Hey God, comparison is stealing my joy. Help me to focus on my journey without looking sideways."

Scripture Reference: "Each of you should test your own actions. Then you can take pride in yourself, without comparing yourself to someone else." —Galatians 6:4

Contemplation: How has comparison impacted your self-esteem?

Daily Reminder: "My journey is my own, and it's beautiful."

Engaging Prompt: Identify one area where you frequently compare yourself to others. How can you shift your focus back to your journey?

My Tender Prayer: "Dear God, may I express my emotions through movement, allowing my body to communicate what words cannot. Amen."

Reflection Prompt: Why does dance feel so reviving and invigorating?

June 7: God, Help Me to Embrace My Story

Prayer: "Jesus, I want to embrace my story, even the messy parts. Help me to see how my past has shaped me for good."

Scripture Reference: "And we know that in all things God works for the good of those who love him." —Romans 8:28

Contemplation: What part of your story are you ready to embrace fully?

Daily Reminder: "My story is a testament to my strength."

Engaging Prompt: Write about a challenge you faced and how it helped you grow.

My Tender Prayer: "God, teach me that there is beauty in stillness as well as movement. Help me find joy in both states. Amen."

Reflection Prompt: Reflect on a time when stillness brought you joy. What did you learn from that experience?

June 8: God, Help Me to Find My Voice

Prayer: "Hey God, I want to find and use my voice boldly. Help me to speak my truth with courage."

Scripture Reference: "For we do not speak as those who are in the world, but as those who are sent by God, declaring His truth with confidence." —2 Corinthians 5:20

Contemplation: How can you express your true self more openly?

Daily Reminder: "My voice matters and deserves to be heard."

Engaging Prompt: Write down your thoughts on a topic that matters to you. Share them with someone you trust.

My Tender Prayer: "Lord, guide me to appreciate the small joys in daily movement—walking, stretching, and breathing deeply. Amen."

Reflection Prompt: Laugh with a friend.

June 9: God, Help Me to Practice Self-Compassion

Prayer: "Jesus, help me to treat myself with the same kindness I offer to others. I need to practice self-compassion."

Scripture Reference: "Be kind and compassionate to one another, forgiving each other, just as in Christ God forgave you." —Ephesians 4:32

Contemplation: What areas of your life need more compassion from you?

Daily Reminder: "I am learning to love myself well."

Engaging Prompt: Write a note to yourself filled with compassion and encouragement.

My Tender Prayer: "Heavenly Father, may I celebrate the uniqueness of my body's movements, recognizing that they are a form of art. Amen."

Reflection Prompt: Can you get a massage today?

June 10: God, Help Me to Own My Feelings

Prayer: "Hey God, sometimes I suppress my feelings instead of owning them. Help me to acknowledge what I feel and express it."

Scripture Reference: "Cast all your anxiety on him because he cares for you." —1 Peter 5:7

Contemplation: What emotions are you holding onto that need to be released?

Daily Reminder: "My feelings are valid and deserve attention."

Engaging Prompt: Journal about a feeling you've been avoiding. What do you want to say about it?

My Tender Prayer: "God, help me embrace the joy of movement as a celebration of life. May I find happiness in every action I take. Amen."

Reflection Prompt: What actions bring you joy in your daily life? Write or draw about a moment of joy you experienced today.

June 11: God, Help Me to Seek Support

Prayer: "Jesus, I know I don't have to carry this weight alone. Help me to open my heart and seek the support of those who lift me up and remind me of my worth. Show me the people who will encourage me, challenge me to grow, and stand by me through it all. Teach me that leaning on others is not a sign of weakness, but a strength that allows me to walk with more courage and grace."

Scripture Reference: "Two are better than one, because they have a good return for their labor." —Ecclesiastes 4:9

Contemplation: Who can you reach out to for support right now?

Daily Reminder: "Support is essential for my journey."

Engaging Prompt: Make a list of people in your life who inspire you. Reach out to one today!

My Tender Prayer: "Lord, may I dance through life with grace and confidence. Teach me to trust my body's ability to express joy. Amen."

Reflection Prompt: Reflect on a time when you felt graceful or confident while moving. How can you carry that feeling into today?

June 12: God, Help Me to Trust the Process

Prayer: "Hey God, I want to trust the process of my growth, even when it feels slow. Help me to have faith in your timing."

Scripture Reference: "Being confident of this, that he who began a good work in you will carry it on to completion." —Philippians 1:6

Contemplation: What aspects of your life do you find hard to trust?

Daily Reminder: "Trusting the process leads to profound growth."

Engaging Prompt: Write down your current goals and the steps you're taking to achieve them. Celebrate each small step!

My Tender Prayer: "Dear God, help me find joy in group activities that allow me to connect with others through movement. Amen."

Reflection Prompt: Is there an event or class that you could attend that would bring you closer to others?

June 13: God, Help Me to See My Worth

Prayer: "Jesus, I often struggle to see my worth. Help me to recognize my inherent value as your creation."

Scripture Reference: "Are not five sparrows sold for two pennies? Yet not one of them is forgotten by God." —Luke 12:6

Contemplation: How do you define your worth?

Daily Reminder: "My worth is not tied to my past or my choices."

Engaging Prompt: Write about what makes you unique and valuable, independent of others' opinions.

My Tender Prayer: "God, guide me to explore different ways to move my body. May I discover new passions in the process. Amen."

Reflection Prompt: What new form of movement have you always wanted to try? Write about your thoughts on exploring it.

June 14: God, help me to Let Go of Fear

Prayer: "Hey God, fear sometimes holds me back from stepping into my true self. Help me to let go of fear and trust your love."

Scripture Reference: "There is no fear in love. But perfect love drives out fear." —1 John 4:18

Contemplation: What fears are keeping you from embracing your true self?

Daily Reminder: "Love casts out my fear."

Engaging Prompt: Write a fear you want to release this month. What steps can you take to overcome it?

My Tender Prayer: "Lord, may I find balance in my life through movement and expression. Help me create harmony within myself. Amen."

Reflection Prompt: What activities bring you balance? Write about how you can integrate them into your life for greater joy.

June 15: God, Help Me to Cultivate Joy

Prayer: "Jesus, I want to cultivate joy that fills every corner of my life. Help me to find happiness in the little things—the sunshine, the laughter, the simple moments that make life beautiful. Teach me to appreciate the small blessings, the quiet victories, and the everyday miracles that often go unnoticed. Let my heart be full of gratitude and joy, no matter what the day brings."

Scripture Reference: "The joy of the Lord is my strength." —Nehemiah 8:10

Contemplation: What brings you joy and how can you incorporate more of it into your life?

Daily Reminder: "Joy is a chance I can make every day."

Engaging Prompt: List three things that make you smile. Do at least one of them today!

My Tender Prayer: "Heavenly Father, help me release any self-judgment that hinders my joy in movement. Teach me to embrace imperfection. Amen."

Reflection Prompt: How does self-judgment affect your movement? Reflect on how you can let go of these thoughts.

June 16: God, Help Me to Love Others Freely

Prayer: "Hey God, help me to love others with an open heart, without holding anything back. I want to be a true source of love, kindness, and support in the lives of those around me. Teach me to love fiercely, with compassion and grace, even when it's hard or uncomfortable. Let my love be a light that lifts others up, a constant reminder of Your goodness. Show me how to pour into others the way You've poured into me."

Scripture Reference: "Above all, love each other deeply, because love covers over a multitude of sins." —1 Peter 4:8

Contemplation: How can you show love to someone today?

Daily Reminder: "Loving freely enriches my life."

Engaging Prompt: Send a message of love and appreciation to a friend or family member today.

My Tender Prayer: "God, guide me to appreciate the connection between my mind, body, and spirit through movement. Amen."

Reflection Prompt: Look at your hands and think of all the things they do for you.

June 17: God, Help Me to Walk in Faith

Prayer: "Jesus, I want to walk in faith, fully trusting Your plan for my life. Even when the road isn't clear, help me to take bold, confident steps forward. Give me the courage to follow where You lead, even if it means stepping out of my comfort zone."

Scripture Reference: "For we live by faith, not by sight." —2 Corinthians 5:7

Contemplation: What area of your life needs a leap of faith?

Daily Reminder: "Faith guides my steps forward."

Engaging Prompt: Identify one step of faith you can take this week. What will it be?

My Tender Prayer: "Lord, help me to see the sacredness in movement, as it reflects the life You've given me. Amen."

Reflection Prompt: Reflect on a movement that feels sacred to you. Write about why it resonates with your spirit.

June 18: God, Help Me to Be Grateful

Prayer: "Hey God, I want to cultivate a heart of gratitude. Help me to focus on the blessings in my life."

Scripture Reference: "Give thanks in all circumstances; for this is God's will for you in Christ Jesus." —1 Thessalonians 5:18

Contemplation: What are you grateful for today?

Daily Reminder: "Gratitude transforms my perspective."

Engaging Prompt: Look for things to appreciate with your eyes.

My Tender Prayer: "Dear God, may I find joy in expressing myself creatively, whether through dance, art, or writing. Amen."

Reflection Prompt: Why does story telling or artwork feel so good?

June 19: God, Help Me to Take Risks

Prayer: "Jesus, help me step out of my comfort zone and take those bold risks that lead to real growth. I don't want to just play it safe; I want to live life with fire and intention. Give me the courage to try new things, to face challenges head-on, and to embrace the unknown with confidence. Let every leap of faith bring me closer to the person You've created me to be, and let me live boldly in Your love and guidance."

Scripture Reference: "Fear not, for I have redeemed you; I have called you by your name, you are mine." —Isaiah 43:1

Contemplation: What risks have you been avoiding?

Daily Reminder: "Taking risks opens the door to new opportunities."

Engaging Prompt: Identify one risk you want to take this month. How will you prepare for it?

My Tender Prayer: "God, help me discover the joy of movement as a spiritual practice. Teach me to honor my body as a temple. Amen."

Reflection Prompt: What movements feel spiritual to you? Write about how they connect you to your faith.

June 20: God, Help Me to Accept Help

Prayer: "Hey God, I know I don't have to do everything alone. Help me to accept help and support when I need it."

Scripture Reference: "Carry each other's burdens, and in this way, you will fulfill the law of Christ." —Galatians 6:2

Contemplation: Are there areas where you could use some support?

Daily Reminder: "Accepting help is a strength, not a weakness."

Engaging Prompt: Reach out to someone today and ask for help with something you're struggling with.

My Tender Prayer: "Lord, may I embrace playful movement that brings laughter and joy into my life. Teach me not to take myself too seriously. Amen."

Reflection Prompt: What playful activities make you laugh? Write about how you can include more playfulness in your routine.

June 21: God, Help Me to Be Present

Prayer: "Jesus, help me to stay in the moment, fully here and now, and not get lost in the what-ifs of the past or the anxious what-abouts of the future. I want to live in the joy of today, soaking up every little blessing, every laugh, every sweet moment. Help me to trust that You've got the past covered and the future in Your hands. Teach me to appreciate where I am, right here, right now, and make the most of it with a grateful heart."

Scripture Reference: "Do not worry about tomorrow, for tomorrow will worry about itself." —Matthew 6:34

Contemplation: How can you practice mindfulness today?

Daily Reminder: "Being present brings peace."

Engaging Prompt: Take a few moments to breathe deeply and focus on your surroundings. What do you notice?

My Tender Prayer: "Heavenly Father, help me to be present in my body during movement. Teach me to savor each moment fully. Amen."

Reflection Prompt: Washing your hair can be spiritual.

June 22: God, Help Me to Stay True to Myself

Prayer: "Hey God, everything's moving fast around me—so many opinions, so many pressures. Help me to stay true to myself and not bend on what I believe, no matter what or who's trying to sway me. Teach me to stand strong in my values and walk with confidence, knowing that You've got my back. Let me stay cool, calm, and authentic, no matter what the world throws my way."

Scripture Reference: "Do not conform to the pattern of this world but be transformed by the renewing of your mind." —Romans 12:2

Contemplation: What values are most important to you?

Daily Reminder: "Staying true to myself is my greatest strength."

Engaging Prompt: Write down your core values and how you can embody them this week.

My Tender Prayer: "God, may I find joy in the process of moving, not just the outcome. Teach me to enjoy the journey. Amen."

Reflection Prompt: What are you currently working toward? Reflect on how you can find joy in the process, not just the result.

June 23: God, Help Me to Forgive Myself

Prayer: "Jesus, sometimes I struggle to forgive myself for my past mistakes. Help me to let go and embrace your grace."

Scripture Reference: "If we confess our sins, he is faithful and just and will forgive us our sins." —1 John 1:9

Contemplation: What do you need to forgive yourself for?

Daily Reminder: "Forgiveness is a gift I can give to myself."

Engaging Prompt: Write a letter of forgiveness to yourself. What do you want to say?

My Tender Prayer: "Lord, help me to move with intention and purpose. Teach me to honor my body's wisdom in every step. Amen."

Reflection Prompt: How can you listen to your body today?

June 24: God, Help Me to Connect with My Community

Prayer: "Hey God, help me connect with the people around me and build real, meaningful relationships. Show me how to show up for my community—whether it's through support, kindness, or just a listening ear. Teach me how to truly see others, to build bonds that are genuine and lasting. Let me be a source of light and love in the lives of those I meet, and help me surround myself with people who lift me up, too

Scripture Reference "Let us consider how we may spur one another on toward love and good deeds." —Hebrews 10:24

Contemplation: Who in your community could use your support or friendship?

Daily Reminder: "Connection enriches my life."

Engaging Prompt: Plan a time to connect with a friend or join a community event this month.

My Tender Prayer: "Dear God, may I appreciate the joy of being alive through every movement I make. Teach me to celebrate life. Amen."

Reflection Prompt: What does it mean to be alive for you? Write about how movement connects you to the experience of living.

June 25: God, Help Me to Focus on the Positive

Prayer: "Jesus, help me shift my focus from the negative and embrace the positive. I want to create space in my heart for gratitude, joy, and all the little pleasures life has to offer. Teach me to look for the silver linings, even when things feel tough, and remind me of the beauty in every moment. Let me cultivate a mindset that celebrates the good, fills me with peace, and keeps my heart light and hopeful."

Scripture Reference: "Finally, brothers and sisters, whatever is true, whatever is noble, whatever is right, whatever is pure, whatever is lovely—think about such things." —Philippians 4:8

Contemplation: What positive thoughts can you hold onto today?

Daily Reminder: "Focusing on the positive changes my perspective."

Engaging Prompt: Write about a recent positive experience. How did it make you feel?

My Tender Prayer: "God, guide me to connect with others through shared movement experiences. Help me build community and joy. Amen."

Reflection Prompt: How can you engage with others through movement? Write about ideas for creating shared experiences.

June 26: God, Help Me to Seek Balance

Prayer: "Hey God, help me to find balance in my life. I could work round the clock, but I want to prioritize my well-being while pursuing my goals."

Scripture Reference: "A person's steps are directed by the Lord. How then can anyone understand their own way?" —Proverbs 20:24

Contemplation: How can you create more balance in your daily life?

Daily Reminder: "Balance is key to my well-being."

Engaging Prompt: List areas of your life that need more balance. What steps can you take to achieve it?

My Tender Prayer: "Lord, help me to find joy in the simplest of movements, reminding me that every action is a blessing. Amen."

Reflection Prompt: Reflect on a simple movement that brings you joy—whether it's stretching, walking, or dancing. Describe that feeling.

June 27: God, Help Me to Embrace Change

Prayer: "Jesus, change can be hard, but I want to embrace it. Help me to see the opportunities in every transition."

Scripture Reference: "Forget the former things; do not dwell on the past. See, I am doing a new thing! Now it springs up; do you not perceive it? I am making a way in the wilderness and streams in the wasteland." —Isaiah 43:18-19

Contemplation: What changes are you currently facing?

Daily Reminder: "Embracing change leads to growth."

Engaging Prompt: Write about a change you're currently experiencing and how you can approach it positively.

My Tender Prayer: "Heavenly Father, may I find the strength to move through challenges with grace. Teach me resilience through movement. Amen."

Reflection Prompt: What challenges have you faced recently? Write about how movement has helped you cope with them.

June 28: God, Help Me to Find My Purpose

Prayer: "Hey God, I'm seeking my purpose in life. Help me to understand the path you've laid out for me."

Scripture Reference: "For I know the plans I have for you, declares the Lord, plans to prosper you and not to harm you, plans to give you hope and a future." —Jeremiah 29:11

Contemplation: What passions ignite your spirit?

Daily Reminder: "My purpose is unfolding in God's perfect timing."

Engaging Prompt: Spend time brainstorming what brings you joy and fulfillment. How can you pursue it further?

My Tender Prayer: "God, help me celebrate my body's ability to move and express joy in whatever form it takes. Amen."

Reflection Prompt: What physical abilities do you appreciate most? Write or draw about how you can celebrate them today.

June 29: God, Help Me to Show Kindness

Prayer: "Jesus, I want to be a kindness powerhouse in this world! Help me drop love and compassion like it's my superpower, spreading good vibes everywhere I go. Teach me to show up for people—no judgment, just pure, real support. Let me be that person who lifts others up, even when the world's a little messy, and remind me that kindness is always in style."

Scripture Reference: "Be kind and compassionate to one another." —Ephesians 4:32

Contemplation: How can you show kindness today?

Daily Reminder: "Kindness has the power to change lives."

Engaging Prompt: Perform a random act of kindness today and write about the experience.

My Tender Prayer: "Lord, may I honor my body's limits and celebrate its capabilities. Teach me to move with gratitude and joy. Amen."

Reflection Prompt: What limits have you learned to accept? Reflect on how this acceptance has changed your experience of movement.

June 30: God, Help Me to Trust in Your Plan

Prayer: "Hey God, it seems like everyone else has it all figured out, even if they really don't. I want to trust in your plan for my life, even when things feel uncertain. Help me to lean on your understanding."

Scripture Reference: "Trust in the Lord with all your heart and lean not on your own understanding." —Proverbs 3:5

Contemplation: What uncertainties are you facing right now?

Daily Reminder: "Trusting God brings peace amidst chaos."

Engaging Prompt: Write about an area where you need to trust God more. How can you take a step of faith in that direction?

My Tender Prayer: "Dear God, thank You for the gift of movement. May I always find joy in expressing my spirit through my body. Amen."

Reflection Prompt: How important is physical fitness to your journey?

Seasonal Message for July, August, September

As we step into the second half of the year, we embrace a powerful season of transformation. The months of July, August, and September invite us to explore the themes of Freedom & Breaking Chains, Authentic Living, and Rest, Contemplation & Reset. This is a time to release the burdens that have weighed us down and to rediscover our true selves.

July: Freedom & Breaking Chains focuses on shedding the limitations we've placed on ourselves, whether from past relationships, societal expectations, or self-doubt. This month encourages us to find our freedom by breaking free from the chains that bind us, allowing us to step boldly into the life God has planned for us.

August: Authentic Living challenges us to embrace our uniqueness. It's about celebrating the quirks, experiences, and journeys that shape who we are. This month empowers us to live authentically, guided by faith and confidence, as we recognize that our imperfections and past experiences contribute to our beautiful narratives.

September: Rest, Reflection & Reset encourages us to slow down and take a breath. As we transition into the fall, we're reminded of the importance of rest and reflection. This month serves as a reminder to pause, recharge, and reset our intentions. It's a time to reflect on our journeys, learn from the past, and prepare our hearts for the seasons ahead.

Together, these months symbolize a journey toward liberation, authenticity, and renewal. Let's embrace this transformative season with open hearts and a willingness to grow, knowing that through prayer and reflection, we can emerge stronger and more empowered than ever before.

July: Freedom & Breaking Chains

July: Freedom & Breaking Chains

As we enter July, it's time to let go of the limitations we've imposed on ourselves—whether they stem from past relationships, societal pressures, or self-doubt. This month invites us to pursue true freedom by breaking the chains that hold us back, empowering us to step confidently into the life God has destined for us. Let's embrace this journey of liberation and discover the strength to move forward with purpose and clarity.

July 1: God, Help Me to Break Free

Prayer: "Hey God, today I'm asking for the strength to break free from anything that holds me back. I'm ready to embrace the freedom you promise!"

Scripture Reference: "It is for freedom that Christ has set us free." —Galatians 5:1

Contemplation: What chains do you want to break this month?

Daily Reminder: "Freedom is my birthright."

Engaging Prompt: Do something out of character for yourself, light-hearted and fun.

My Tender Prayer: "God, fill me with the confidence to stand tall in my truth. Help me honor my needs and set boundaries with love. Amen."

Reflection Prompt: What does confidence mean to you? Write or draw about a time you felt truly confident.

July 2: God, Help Me to Let Go of Guilt

Prayer: "Jesus, help me to let go of the guilt I carry. I know you've forgiven me, so it's time I forgive myself. People have made awful assumptions about my character. Yes, it was based on some reckless behavior, but that doesn't really reflect my genuine nature. And even though I know it is not true, I feel the need to prove to them, whomever they are, that I AM a good person. But they measure me not by an average of deeds, but rather by whatever situations they don't understand."

Scripture Reference: "As far as the east is from the west, so far has he removed our transgressions from us." —Psalm 103:12

Contemplation: What guilt do you need to release?

Daily Reminder: "Letting go of guilt opens the door to joy."

Engaging Prompt: Write a letter to yourself about your feelings of guilt and then tear it up.

My Tender Prayer: "Lord, teach me to recognize my worth. Help me see that I deserve respect and love just as I am. Amen."

Reflection Prompt: What qualities do you appreciate about yourself? Write them down and reflect on why they matter.

July 3: God, Help Me to Embrace Change

Prayer: "Hey God, stepping into the unknown feels like walking without a map, but I trust You to guide me. I used to think my worth was measured by the eyes on me and the stories I could tell. Now, I realize You have something deeper and truer for me. Show me how to walk with confidence into this new chapter and see the beauty in the woman You are shaping me to be."

Scripture Reference: ""Do not conform to the pattern of this world, but be transformed by the renewing of your mind. Then you will be able to test and approve what God's will is—his good, pleasing and perfect will." — Romans 12:2

Contemplation: What changes are you facing that you need to embrace?

Daily Reminder: "Change is the catalyst for growth."

Engaging Prompt: Call a friend and talk about how things have changed.

My Tender Prayer: "Heavenly Father, guide me in learning to say no when I need to. Help me honor my boundaries without guilt. Amen."

Reflection Prompt: Reflect on a time you struggled to say no. What could you have done differently?

July 4: God, Help Me to Seek Forgiveness

Prayer: "Jesus, I know I've made mistakes and hurt others, including myself. Please help me to take the steps needed to heal those wounds, even when it's hard. Teach me humility to seek forgiveness, courage to make amends, and grace to forgive myself. Show me how to rebuild what's been broken and bring peace where there's been division."

Scripture Reference: "Forgive us our debts, as we also have forgiven our debtors." —Matthew 6:12

Contemplation: Who do you need to ask for forgiveness?

Daily Reminder: "Forgiveness heals my heart."

Engaging Prompt: Consider reaching out to someone to express your regret and seek forgiveness.

My Tender Prayer: "God, grant me the courage to express my needs and desires openly. May I communicate with clarity and confidence. Amen."

Reflection Prompt: Find the words for your desires.

July 5: God, Help Me to Release Fear

Prayer: "Hey God, I want to release my fears. I've worried about so many things have never ended up happening, that I think my imagination was running wild. Help me to trust that you're in control and have my back."

Scripture Reference: "For God has not given us a spirit of fear, but of power, love, and a sound mind." —2 Timothy 1:7

Contemplation: What fears are clouding your judgement?

Daily Reminder: "Fear doesn't define me."

Engaging Prompt: Write down one fear you want to overcome and how you plan to face it.

My Tender Prayer: "Lord, help me create healthy boundaries that protect my energy and well-being while still being able to find pleasure in moments with others. Teach me to prioritize myself. Amen."

Reflection Prompt: Where can you be fearless in your life?

July 6: God, Help Me to Stand in My Power

Prayer: "Jesus, help me to step fully into my power and own it. I know there's so much more within me than I've even realized, and I'm ready to unleash it. Teach me to trust in my strength, my abilities, and the incredible potential You've placed inside me. Help me stand tall, confident, and ready to take on whatever comes my way, knowing that with You by my side, I'm capable of anything."

Scripture Reference: "I can do all this through him who gives me strength." —Philippians 4:13

Contemplation: What strengths do you possess that you haven't fully embraced?

Daily Reminder: "I am powerful and capable."

Engaging Prompt: List three things you're proud of accomplishing this year.

My Tender Prayer: "Dear God, remind me that it's okay to take up space and to have desires. Help me embrace my presence in this world. Amen."

Reflection Prompt: What does take up space mean to you? Write about how you can honor your presence today.

July 7: God, Help Me to Prioritize My Well-Being

Prayer: "Hey God, I have been focused on everyone else for so very long, that I hardly ever take care of me. I want to prioritize my well-being, both mentally and physically. Help me to take care of myself."

Scripture Reference: "Do you not know that your bodies are temples of the Holy Spirit?" —1 Corinthians 6:19

Contemplation: How can you better prioritize your well-being?

Daily Reminder: "My well-being is important."

Engaging Prompt: Plan a self-care activity for this week. What will you do?

My Tender Prayer: "God, help me let go of comparisons to others. Teach me to appreciate my unique journey and strengths. Amen."

Reflection Prompt: How does comparing yourself to others affect your confidence? Reflect on ways to embrace your individuality.

July 8: God, Help Me to Seek Community

Prayer: "Jesus, I want to surround myself with the kind of people who lift me up, inspire me, and push me to be my best. Help me seek out community, not just for connection, but for real, authentic relationships that fill me with joy and growth. Guide me to those who share my energy, who encourage me to dream big, and who make me feel seen and supported. Let me build a circle that truly brings out the best in me—and in others."

Scripture Reference: "For where two or three gather in my name, there am I with them." —Matthew 18:20

Contemplation: Who in your life uplifts you?

Daily Reminder: "Community supports my growth."

Engaging Prompt: Reach out to a friend and plan a time to connect this week.

My Tender Prayer: "Lord, may I find strength in vulnerability. Help me understand that being open can lead to deeper connections. Amen."

Reflection Prompt: When have you felt vulnerable yet strong? Write about that experience and what it taught you.

July 9: God, Help Me to Find My Voice

Prayer: "Hey God, I want to find my voice and speak my truth loud and clear. Help me share my story with confidence, without holding back, but also with the wisdom to know when to keep things just for me. Guide me to express myself in a way that's real, authentic, and not afraid to be bold, but also balanced and respectful. Let me speak with love and strength, knowing that my truth is worth sharing."

Scripture Reference: "Let your yes be yes, and your no be no." —Matthew 5:37

Contemplation: What truth have you been hesitant to share?

Daily Reminder: "My voice matters."

Engaging Prompt: Write about something you believe in strongly and how you can express it.

My Tender Prayer: "Heavenly Father, help me recognize when my boundaries are being tested. Give me the wisdom to respond with grace. Amen."

Reflection Prompt: Think of a time when someone crossed your boundaries. How did you respond, and what would you do differently now?

July 10: God, Help Me to Celebrate My Journey

Prayer: "Jesus, I've carried the weight of my mistakes for too long. I want to make things right—with others and with myself. Give me the words and the courage to reach out and the humility to admit where I went wrong. Help me to rebuild trust and show love, even in small steps. Teach me how to forgive myself so I can move forward with peace in my heart."

Scripture Reference: "Who is a God like you, who pardons sin and forgives the transgression of the remnant of his inheritance? You do not stay angry forever but delight to show mercy. You will again have compassion on us; you will tread our sins underfoot and hurl all our iniquities into the depths of the sea." — Micah 7:18-19

Contemplation: What milestones have you achieved recently?

Daily Reminder: "Every step in my journey is worth celebrating."

Engaging Prompt: Plan a small celebration for yourself this month. What will it be?

My Tender Prayer: "God, help me surround myself with people who respect my boundaries and uplift my spirit. Amen."

Reflection Prompt: Who in your life supports your boundaries? Write about how you can deepen those relationships.

July 11: God, Help Me to Set Boundaries

Prayer: "Hey God, I want to set healthy boundaries in my life. Help me to prioritize my needs without feeling guilty."

Scripture Reference: "No one can serve two masters. Either you will hate the one and love the other, or you will be devoted to the one and despise the other." —Matthew 6:24

Contemplation: What boundaries do you need to establish?

Daily Reminder: "Setting boundaries is an act of self-love."

Engaging Prompt: Identify the feelings associated with having your boundaries crossed.

My Tender Prayer: "Lord, may I cultivate confidence in my abilities and trust that I am capable of achieving my goals. Amen."

Reflection Prompt: What achievements are you proud of? Reflect on how these successes can fuel your confidence moving forward.

July 12: God, Help Me to Recognize My Worth

Prayer: "Jesus, sometimes I hide my brilliance, sometimes I doubt my shine. help me to recognize my worth and value. I am deserving of love and respect."

Scripture Reference: "You are precious in my sight, and honored, and I love you." —Isaiah 43:4

Contemplation: How can you remind yourself of your worth?

Daily Reminder: "I am worthy of love and respect."

Engaging Prompt: Write down five qualities that make you uniquely you.

My Tender Prayer: "Dear God, help me to trust my instincts and faith. May I listen to my inner voice with confidence. Amen."

Reflection Prompt: What do you want?

July 13: God, Help Me to Trust the Process

Prayer: "Hey God, it occurred to me that stress is often pointless. I want to trust the process of life. Help me to have faith that everything will unfold as it should."

Scripture Reference: "Commit your way to the Lord; trust in him, and he will act." — Psalm 37:5

Contemplation: What process do you find difficult to trust?

Daily Reminder: "Trusting the process leads to peace."

Engaging Prompt: Identify one area of your life where you need to practice patience.

My Tender Prayer: "God, may I approach challenges with a confident mindset. Help me see obstacles as opportunities for growth. Amen."

Reflection Prompt: What do you feel?

July 14: God, Help Me to See the Beauty in the Journey

Prayer: "Jesus, help me to see the beauty in my life, in my body, in my journey, even when the path is tough and I just rolled out of bed."

Scripture Reference: "Count it all joy, my brothers, when you meet trials of various kinds." —James 1:2

Contemplation: What moments of beauty have stayed with you, lasting memories of dew drops or sun roses, or the laughter of a stranger?

Daily Reminder: "I am Beautiful"

Engaging Prompt: Call a friend, bonus points if you talk about a challenging experience that taught you something valuable.

My Tender Prayer: "Lord, teach me to celebrate my victories, no matter how small. Help me recognize the progress I make each day. Amen."

Reflection Prompt: Make your favorite meal or treat.

July 15: God, Help Me to Speak Life

Prayer: "Hey God, help me be careful in the way I speak to myself. Lord, help me to speak life into my dreams, instead of my fears, and help me to choose words that inspire the dreams of others. Words have power!"

Scripture Reference: "Death and life are in the power of the tongue." —Proverbs 18:21

Contemplation: How can you use your words to uplift others?

Daily Reminder: "My words affect others."

Engaging Prompt: Write a note of encouragement to someone you care about.

My Tender Prayer: "Heavenly Father, may I let go of the need for perfection. Teach me that growth comes from embracing imperfection. Amen."

Reflection Prompt: How does the pursuit of perfection affect your confidence? Write about the beauty of being imperfect.

July 16: God, Help Me to Be Present

Prayer: "Jesus, I want to be fully present in my life. Help me to focus on today and not get lost in the past or future."

Scripture Reference: "Therefore do not worry about tomorrow, for tomorrow will worry about itself." —Matthew 6:34

Contemplation: What distractions keep you from being present?

Daily Reminder: "Today is a gift; I will cherish it."

Engaging Prompt: Spend 10 minutes in silence today, focusing on your breath and being present.

My Tender Prayer: "God, help me learn to ask for help when I need it. May I understand that seeking support is a sign of strength. Amen."

Reflection Prompt: When have you hesitated to ask for help? Reflect on how reaching out could strengthen your confidence.

July 17: God, Help Me to Appreciate My Support System

Prayer: "Hey God, I am not always the kindest to those who are close to me. Sometimes I cater to new friends or fleeting encounters more than I do existing relationships in my life. Help me to appreciate the people who support me. I am grateful for their love and encouragement."

Scripture Reference: "I thank my God every time I remember you." —Philippians 1:3

Contemplation: Who in your life offers you support?

Daily Reminder: "I am never alone."

Engaging Prompt: Reach out to someone in your support system and express your gratitude.

My Tender Prayer: "Lord, may I find strength in community. Help me build connections that inspire and uplift me. Amen."

Reflection Prompt: What communities or groups bring you joy? Write about how they contribute to your confidence.

July 18: God, Help Me to Release Toxic Relationships

Prayer: "Jesus, help me see clearly the relationships in my life that aren't serving my growth or peace. Give me the strength to let go of anything toxic, no matter how hard it feels, and remind me that I deserve connections that are healthy, uplifting, and full of love. Teach me to set boundaries with grace and seek out relationships that reflect Your goodness and support my journey."

Scripture Reference: "Do not be deceived: 'Bad company corrupts good character.'" —1 Corinthians 15:33

Contemplation: What relationships drain your energy?

Daily Reminder: "I deserve healthy relationships."

Engaging Prompt: Make a list of relationships that uplift you and those that drain you.

My Tender Prayer: "Dear God, help me embrace my uniqueness. Teach me that my differences are what make me special. Amen."

Reflection Prompt: What unique traits do you possess? Write about how they contribute to your confidence and sense of self.

July 19: God, Help Me to Cultivate Joy

Prayer: "Hey God, I want to fill my life with joy—the kind that shows up in the little things: a warm smile, a good laugh, or the way the sun feels on my skin. Help me let go of anything that weighs me down and open my heart to the simple, beautiful moments You've sprinkled all around me. Teach me to find happiness right here, right now."

Scripture Reference: "The joy of the Lord is your strength." —Nehemiah 8:10

Contemplation: What brings you joy?

Daily Reminder: "Joy is my choice."

Engaging Prompt: List three things that bring you joy and make time for them this week.

My Tender Prayer: "God, May I honor my emotions and understand that they do not diminish my confidence. Amen."

Reflection Prompt: How do you handle your emotions? Reflect on how embracing them can enhance your confidence.

July 20: God, Help Me to Practice Gratitude

Prayer: "Jesus, help me to practice gratitude daily. I want to see the blessings in my life."

Scripture Reference: "Give thanks in all circumstances; for this is the will of God." —1 Thessalonians 5:18

Contemplation: What are you thankful for today?

Daily Reminder: "Gratitude shifts my perspective."

Engaging Prompt: Tell others what you appreciate about them.

My Tender Prayer: "Lord, help me set clear intentions for my life. Teach me that clarity fosters confidence in my decisions. Amen."

Reflection Prompt: What kind of goals do I really want to set for myself?

July 21: God, Help Me to Be Vulnerable

Prayer: "Hey God, I want to embrace vulnerability. Help me to share my true self with those I trust."

Scripture Reference: "Confess your faults one to another, and pray one for another, that ye may be healed." —James 5:16

Contemplation: What does vulnerability mean to you?

Daily Reminder: "Being vulnerable is a strength."

Engaging Prompt: Share a personal story with a trusted friend or family member.

My Tender Prayer: "Heavenly Father, guide me to practice self-compassion. Help me be gentle with myself on this journey. Amen."

Reflection Prompt: How can you practice self-compassion today? Reflect on ways to treat yourself kindly.

July 22: God, Help Me to Set Intentions

Prayer: Jesus, I want to set intentions that align with who I am and what truly matters. Help me to focus on the things that bring meaning, joy, and purpose to my life. Clear away the distractions and show me how to prioritize what's real and lasting."

Scripture Reference: "Commit to the Lord whatever you do, and he will establish your plans." —Proverbs 16:3

Contemplation: What intentions do you want to set for this month?

Daily Reminder: "My intentions shape my plans."

Engaging Prompt: Write down three intentions you want to focus on this month.

My Tender Prayer: "God, help me find joy in the unique, vibrant woman You've created me to be. Teach me that embracing every curve, every quirk, and every part of my individuality is the secret to true confidence. Let me feel the beauty of my essence, the power of my sensuality, and the strength in fully owning who I am. Guide me to celebrate myself with grace, love, and pride, knowing that You delight in every bit of me. Amen."

Reflection Prompt: How do you know what you want?

July 23: God, Help Me to Discover My Passion

Prayer: "Hey God, I'm not sure where to start sometimes. I want to level up and move beyond the busy work. I want to discover and pursue my passions. Help me to follow my heart."

Scripture Reference: "Delight yourself in the Lord, and he will give you the desires of your heart." —Psalm 37:4

Contemplation: What are you passionate about?

Daily Reminder: "My passions are a part of my purpose."

Engaging Prompt: Spend time this week engaging in an activity that brings you joy.

My Tender Prayer: "Lord, may I approach new experiences with curiosity and confidence. Help me embrace the unknown. Amen."

Reflection Prompt: What new experience are you considering? Reflect on how you can approach it with an open mind.

July 24: God, Help Me to Be Open to New Experiences

Prayer: "Jesus, help me to get out and about, to go places so that I can be open to new experiences and opportunities. I want to embrace growth."

Scripture Reference: "In their hearts humans plan their course, but the Lord establishes their steps." — Proverbs 16:9

Contemplation: What new experiences have you been avoiding?

Daily Reminder: "New experiences lead to growth."

Engaging Prompt: Try something new this week—whether it's a new hobby, food, or activity!

My Tender Prayer: "Dear God, help me to see challenges as opportunities for growth. May I approach them with a confident heart. Amen."

Reflection Prompt: What if you could do anything?

July 25: God, Help Me to Shine My Light

Prayer: "Hey God, help me to shine my light brightly in the world. I want to be a source of love and positivity."

Scripture Reference: "You are the light of the world. A town built on a hill cannot be hidden." —Matthew 5:14

Contemplation: How can you shine your light today?

Daily Reminder: "My light can change the world."

Engaging Prompt: Perform an act of kindness for someone today.

My Tender Prayer: "God, may I learn to forgive myself for past mistakes. Teach me that my worth is not defined by my failures. Amen."

Reflection Prompt: What past mistakes do you need to forgive yourself for? Reflect on how this forgiveness can change your life.

July 26: God, Help Me to Be Patient

Prayer: "Jesus, help me to be patient with myself and others. Growth takes time, and I want to trust the journey."

Scripture Reference: "Patience is better than pride." —Ecclesiastes 7:8

Contemplation: What area of your life requires more patience?

Daily Reminder: "Patience is a virtue."

Engaging Prompt: Practice mindfulness today—take a moment to breathe and enjoy the present.

My Tender Prayer: "Lord, help me stand firm in my beliefs and values. Teach me that confidence comes from authenticity. Amen."

Reflection Prompt: What beliefs and values are important to you? Write about how they shape your confidence.

July 27: God, Help Me to Seek Wisdom

Prayer: ""Hey God, I come to You with a heart that seeks clarity and purpose. Please guide me to make decisions rooted in wisdom and grace. Help me to pause, listen, and trust Your voice above my own desires or fears. Align my choices with Your will so that I can walk the path You've laid out for me, confidently and faithfully. When the way seems uncertain, remind me that Your plans are always for my good, and give me the courage to follow where You lead. Amen."

Scripture Reference: "If any of you lacks wisdom, you should ask God, who gives generously to all without finding fault." —James 1:5

Contemplation: Where do you need wisdom right now?

Daily Reminder: "Wisdom guides my steps."

Engaging Prompt: Spend time reading a book or article that inspires you and provides insight.

My Tender Prayer: "Heavenly Father, may I approach difficult conversations with confidence and grace. Teach me to speak my truth. Amen."

Reflection Prompt: What difficult conversation are you avoiding? Reflect on how you can prepare to approach it confidently.

July 28: God, Help Me to Trust in Your Plan

Prayer: "Dear Jesus, You created me with a body, heart, and spirit that reflect Your image. Help me to embrace the beauty and wonder of my sensuality as a gift from You. Teach me to honor this part of myself in a way that celebrates the love, joy, and creativity You've designed.

Guide me to live with integrity, keeping my faith at the center of all I do. Let my confidence and self-expression flow from the truth of Your love, not the world's fleeting standards. Help me to balance the sacred and the sensual, knowing that both can glorify You when rooted in grace and wisdom.

May I walk in the fullness of who You've created me to be, holding my faith as my foundation while embracing the divine beauty of my womanhood. Amen."

Scripture Reference: "You are altogether beautiful, my darling; there is no flaw in you." — Song of Solomon 4:7

Contemplation: What aspects of your life require more trust in God's plan?

Daily Reminder: "I trust in God's perfect plan."

Engaging Prompt: Write a prayer of surrender, releasing your worries to God.

My Tender Prayer: "God, help me build resilience through challenges. Teach me that each setback is a setup for a comeback. Amen."

Reflection Prompt: Reflect on a setback you faced. How did you bounce back, and what did you learn about resilience?

July 29: God, Help Me to Appreciate My Growth

Prayer: "Hey God, help me to appreciate how far I've come. I want to celebrate my growth and progress."

Scripture Reference: "I am confident of this: that he who began a good work in you will carry it on to completion." —Philippians 1:6

Contemplation: How have you grown this year?

Daily Reminder: "My growth is a testament to God's grace."

Engaging Prompt: Reflect on a challenge you've overcome and how it has shaped you.

My Tender Prayer: "Lord, may I embrace my body as it is today. Teach me to appreciate its strength and beauty. Amen."

Reflection Prompt: What do you love about your body? Write or draw about its unique qualities and strengths.

July 30: God, Help Me to Embrace My Journey

Prayer: "Jesus, my story is like a rollercoaster. Help me to embrace my journey with all its ups and downs. Every experience is part of my story."

Scripture Reference: "Every good gift and every perfect gift is from above." —James 1:17

Contemplation: What have you learned from your journey so far?

Daily Reminder: "My journey is beautiful, and I embrace it."

Engaging Prompt: look at a photo of yourself from five years ago.

My Tender Prayer: "Dear God, thank You for the confidence I've cultivated this month. Help me carry it forward into all aspects of my life. Amen."

Reflection Prompt: Write a letter to your future self about where you hope to be in a year.

July 31: God, Help Me to Move Forward with Faith

Prayer: "Hey God, nothing deep and introspective today, as this month comes to a close, help me to move forward with faith and confidence. I trust in your guidance."

Scripture Reference: "Faith is the assurance of things hoped for, the conviction of things not seen." —Hebrews 11:1

Contemplation: Where were you this time last year?

Daily Reminder: "I move forward in faith."

Engaging Prompt: Set one actionable goal for the coming month that aligns with your faith journey.

My Tender Prayer: "Lord, help me release the fear of judgment. Let me walk with confidence, knowing I am enough just as I am. Amen."

Reflection Prompt: Reflect on a moment you doubted yourself. How can you shift that narrative to one of acceptance?

August: Authentic Living

August calls us to fully embrace the beauty of our individuality. It's a celebration of the quirks, experiences, and journeys that make us who we are. This month encourages us to live boldly and authentically, rooted in faith and self-assurance. By recognizing that our imperfections and past experiences are integral parts of our story, we find the freedom to show up as our true selves. August is about honoring the person God created us to be—flaws and all—and trusting that our unique journey is part of a greater, beautiful narrative.

Welcome to August, a month dedicated to Authentic Living! This is our time to strip away the masks, embrace our true selves, and live life unapologetically. It's about discovering and honoring who we are at our core—beyond the expectations of others and societal pressures. This month encourages us to express our uniqueness and embody our truth.

August 1: God, Help Me to Embrace My True Self

Prayer: "Hey God, today As I look in the mirror, I ask for the courage to embrace who I truly am. Help me to shed the layers that don't reflect my authentic self."

Scripture Reference: "Before I formed you in the womb, I knew you." —Jeremiah 1:5

Contemplation: What parts of yourself have you hidden away?

Daily Reminder: "I am worthy of being my true self."

Engaging Prompt: Write down three qualities that define your authentic self.

My Tender Prayer: "God, I invite healing into my life. Help me release what no longer serves me and embrace renewal. Amen."

Reflection Prompt: What areas of your life need healing? Write or draw about what renewal looks like for you.

August 2: God, Help Me to Celebrate My Uniqueness

Prayer: "Jesus, help me to celebrate my uniqueness and the special gifts you've given me. I want to shine brightly!"

Scripture Reference: "Each of you should use whatever gift you have received to serve others." —1 Peter 4:10

Contemplation: What unique qualities do you bring to the world?

Daily Reminder: "My uniqueness is me."

Engaging Prompt: List five things that make you uniquely you.

My Tender Prayer: "Lord, grant me the strength to face my wounds. May I find courage in the healing process. Amen."

Reflection Prompt: Reflect on a wound you've carried. How can you begin to heal it today?

August 3: God, Help Me to Live My Truth

Prayer: "Hey God, help me to live my truth boldly and unapologetically. I want to be authentic in every aspect of my life. I know I will find remarkable things happening in my life when I can live unapologetically true to my faith in my place in this world."

Scripture Reference: "Let your yes be yes, and your no be no." —Matthew 5:37

Contemplation: Where in your life are you not living your truth?

Daily Reminder: "Living authentically brings peace."

Engaging Prompt: Identify one area where you can start being more authentic.

My Tender Prayer: "Heavenly Father, help me cultivate patience with myself as I heal. Teach me that healing is a journey, not a destination. Amen."

Reflection Prompt: Why do you feel the need to rush yourself?

August 4: God, Help Me to Set Healthy Boundaries

Prayer: "Jesus, teach me to value myself as You value me. Help me to set boundaries that protect my peace, honor my needs, and nurture my authentic self as You created me to be. Give me the strength to say no when necessary and the wisdom to recognize relationships and situations that align with Your will for my life. Let my boundaries reflect my worth as Your beloved and create space for growth, healing, and love rooted in Your truth. May I guard my heart without fear, trusting You to guide me in building a life that guides me. Amen."

Scripture Reference: "The fruit of that righteousness will be peace; its effect will be quietness and confidence forever. My people will live in peaceful dwelling places, in secure homes, in undisturbed places of rest." — Isaiah 32:17-18

Contemplation: What boundaries do you need to establish to protect your authenticity?

Daily Reminder: "Boundaries ensure my needs can be met."

Engaging Prompt: Write down one boundary you want to set this month.

My Tender Prayer: "God, may I learn to let go of the past and embrace the present moment. Help me find peace in the here and now. Amen."

Reflection Prompt: What holds you back from living in the present? Write about how you can release these attachments.

August 5: God, Help Me to Find My Voice

Prayer: "Hey God, there are times when I know I should say something, but I go with the crowd. I want to find my voice and express my thoughts and feelings freely. Help me to speak up for myself."

Scripture Reference: "Open your mouth for the mute, for the rights of all who are destitute." —Proverbs 31:8

Contemplation: What prevents you from expressing your true feelings?

Daily Reminder: "My voice matters."

Engaging Prompt: Share your opinion on a topic that's important to you with someone you trust.

My Tender Prayer: "Lord, guide me to care for the whole of who I am—my body, mind, and spirit. Teach me to see self-care not as indulgence, but as a sacred act of renewal. Help me to listen to what I need, to rest when I'm weary, and to nourish every part of myself with love and intention. Let me honor this vessel You've given me, finding balance and peace in every moment of care. Amen."

Reflection Prompt: What self-care practices help you feel renewed? Write about how you can incorporate them into your routine.

August 6: God, Help Me to Embrace Vulnerability

Prayer: "Jesus, help me see vulnerability for what it truly is—a beautiful, raw strength. Teach me to be open and honest about my feelings, even when it feels scary or uncertain. Show me that sharing my heart doesn't make me weak; it makes me brave. Guide me to trust in the power of authenticity, knowing that being real opens the door to deeper connections and healing."

Scripture Reference: "Confess your faults one to another and pray one for another." —James 5:16

Contemplation: What is the worst thing that could happen by being vulnerable in a normal day to day situation?

Daily Reminder: "Vulnerability connects me to others."

Engaging Prompt: Consider sharing a personal story with someone you trust.

My Tender Prayer: "Dear God, teach me to forgive myself and others. May forgiveness led to healing and freedom in my heart. Amen."

Reflection Prompt: What do you need to forgive yourself for? Reflect on how forgiveness can bring healing.

August 7: God, Help Me to Let Go of Comparison

Prayer: "Hey God, I come before You today, ready to release the weight of comparison that I've been carrying. Help me to embrace my own unique journey with grace and gratitude, knowing that You've guided every step along the way. I've made choices, some good and some not-so-good, and I acknowledge my past—especially the parts that were messy or misunderstood—but I also know that You have redeemed me and made me whole.

Help me to see my past through Your eyes, not as shameful or regretful, but as a collection of lessons that have shaped who I am today. I no longer want to compare my story to anyone else's. I want to honor my body, my experiences, and my future by choosing wisely, by walking in Your love, and by making decisions that reflect Your purpose for my life.

God, give me the strength to move forward in a way that aligns with my values, to honor my sensuality with responsibility and self-respect. Teach me to set boundaries that protect my heart while allowing me to love deeply and freely in ways that glorify You. I trust You to guide me toward the relationships and choices that will bring me peace, joy, and fulfillment, all while honoring the woman You created me to be. Amen."

Scripture Reference: "Each of you should test your own actions. Then you can take pride in yourself alone, without comparing yourself to someone else." —Galatians 6:4

Contemplation: How does comparison affect your self-image?

Daily Reminder: "I am on my own unique journey."

Engaging Prompt: Write down three things you love about your journey, separate from others.

My Tender Prayer: "God, help me to embrace the lessons woven into my past, especially those shaped by love, passion, and longing. Let me honor those experiences, not with regret, but with gratitude for how they've shaped me into the woman I am today. Guide me toward healing that nurtures my soul and growth that awakens my strength. Teach me to carry my past with grace, using it to fuel a future full of self-love, joy, and purpose."

Reflection Prompt: Draw an image of your new understanding of your past.

August 8: God, Help Me to Practice Self-Acceptance

Prayer: "Jesus, I come to You with an open heart, longing to accept myself just as I am. I've often struggled with the parts of me that I've deemed imperfect, flawed, or unworthy. Help me to see myself through Your eyes, knowing that You love me deeply, even in my imperfections. I want to embrace every part of me—the parts that shine with beauty and strength, and the parts that carry hurt, mistakes, and struggles.

Teach me to love myself with the same grace that You've shown me, to let go of self-criticism and judgment, and to understand that I am fearfully and wonderfully made. I know that my flaws do not diminish my worth in Your eyes, but are opportunities for growth, healing, and greater reliance on Your love.

Give me the courage to let go of comparison, to stop measuring myself against others' standards, and to rest in the truth that I am enough because You have created me exactly as You intended. Help me to honor my body, my emotions, my past, and my future, embracing all of it as part of Your beautiful, unique creation. May I walk forward in peace, knowing that I am loved and accepted by You, flaws and all. Amen."

Scripture Reference: "I praise you because I am fearfully and wonderfully made." —Psalm 139:14

Contemplation: What parts of yourself do you struggle to accept?

Daily Reminder: "I am perfect just as I am."

Engaging Prompt: How does vulnerability contribute to your healing? Write about a time you felt empowered by sharing your story.

My Tender Prayer: "Lord, may I discover the strength hidden within my vulnerability. Teach me to share my story with an open heart, embracing every raw and beautiful part of it. Let my words create connections that heal, inspire, and empower others on their own journeys. Show me how to use my experiences, my sensuality, and my truth to foster growth and love—for myself and those around me. Amen.

Reflection Prompt: Write a love letter to yourself, celebrating who you are.

August 9: God, Help Me to Align with My Values

Prayer: "Hey God, help me to align my actions with my values. I want to live authentically according to what I believe."

Scripture Reference: "Let your light shine before others, that they may see your good deeds and glorify your Father in heaven." —Matthew 5:16

Contemplation: What values are most important to you?

Daily Reminder: "My values guide my actions."

Engaging Prompt: List your top three values and reflect on how you can embody them more in your life.

My Tender Prayer: "Heavenly Father, guide me to embrace a circle of supportive and uplifting souls who celebrate my femininity and nurture my spirit. Surround me with those whose love and energy encourage my healing, inspire my growth, and honor the beauty within me. Teach me to welcome connections that enrich my life, allowing their care to deepen my sense of self-love, strength, and sensuality. Amen."

Reflection Prompt: Who in your life supports your healing journey? Reflect on how you can strengthen those connections.

August 10: God, Help Me to Seek Joy in Authenticity

Prayer: "Jesus, help me to seek joy in living authentically. I want to find happiness in being true to myself. Let me love the lighthearted joy of being myself"

Scripture Reference: "But God demonstrates his own love for us in this: While we were still sinners, Christ died for us." — Romans 5:8

Contemplation: What brings you joy when you're being your true self?

Daily Reminder: "Joy comes from living authentically."

Engaging Prompt: Plan an activity this week that brings you joy, reflecting your authentic self.

My Tender Prayer: "God, may I find beauty in the process of healing. Teach me to appreciate each step of the journey. Amen."

Reflection Prompt: What aspects of healing do you find beautiful? Write or draw about the positive changes you've experienced.

August 11: God, Help Me to Surround Myself with Authentic People

Prayer: "Hey God, sometimes hanging with the same crew means doing the same old things. Lord, help me to surround myself with authentic people who uplift and inspire me."

Scripture Reference: "Let us consider how we may spur one another on toward love and good deeds, not giving up meeting together, as some are in the habit of doing, but encouraging one another." —Hebrews 10:24-25

Contemplation: Who in your life encourages you to be your true self?

Daily Reminder: "I am worthy of uplifting connections."

Engaging Prompt: Reach out to someone who inspires you and express your appreciation.

My Tender Prayer: "Lord, help me connect with my emotions and honor them as part of my healing process. Amen."

Reflection Prompt: What emotions have you been avoiding? Reflect on how you can safely express them today.

August 12: God, Help Me to Express My Creativity

Prayer: "Jesus, help me to express my creativity freely. I want to explore my artistic side and share it with the world."

Scripture Reference: "For we are God's handiwork, created in Christ Jesus to do good works, which God prepared in advance for us to do."— Ephesians 2:10

Contemplation: How do you express your creativity?

Daily Reminder: "Creativity flows from my authentic self."

Engaging Prompt: Try a new creative activity this week—painting, writing, or dancing!

My Tender Prayer: "Dear God, help me to embrace my femininity as a gift from You. Teach me to honor and celebrate the unique beauty, strength, and wisdom that reside within me as a woman. Guide me in nurturing my body, heart, and spirit with love and respect. Amen."

Reflection Prompt: How can you express your womanhood with confidence and grace?

August 13: God, Help Me to Live with Intention

Prayer: "Hey God, is life supposed to be meaningful, or meaningfully led? Lord, help me to live with intention and purpose. I want each day to reflect my authentic self."

Scripture Reference: "Commit to the Lord whatever you do, and he will establish your plans." —Proverbs 16:3

Contemplation: What intentions can you set for living authentically.

Daily Reminder: "Living with intention empowers me."

Engaging Prompt: Call a friend and ask them about their goals.

My Tender Prayer: "God, may I trust the timing of my healing journey. Help me embrace each moment as it comes. Amen."

Reflection Prompt: How does trusting the timing of your healing change your perspective? Reflect on the importance of patience.

August 14: God, Help Me to Seek Growth

Prayer: "Jesus, I want to seek growth and learning in my life. Help me to embrace challenges as opportunities for authenticity."

Scripture Reference: "Consider it pure joy, my brothers and sisters, whenever you face trials of many kinds." —James 1:2

Contemplation: What challenges have led to personal growth for you?

Daily Reminder: "Growth is a part of my authentic journey."

Engaging Prompt: Reflect on a recent challenge and what you learned about yourself.

My Tender Prayer: "Lord, help me explore my inner landscape. Teach me to listen to my heart and understand its needs. Amen."

Reflection Prompt: What does your heart need right now? Write about how you can honor those needs.

August 15: God, Help Me to Let Go of the Past

Prayer: "Hey God, help me to let go of my past and move forward with confidence. I want to embrace who I am becoming."

Scripture Reference: "I press on toward the goal to win the prize for which God has called me heavenward in Christ Jesus." —Philippians 3:14

Contemplation: What past experiences are you holding onto that hinder your authenticity?

Daily Reminder: "Letting go frees my spirit."

Engaging Prompt: Write a letter to your past self, thanking them for the lessons learned and then release the stress from the past.

My Tender Prayer: "Heavenly Father, help me reconnect with my dreams and aspirations. May they inspire my healing and renewal. Amen."

Reflection Prompt: What dreams have you set aside? Reflect on how you can start pursuing them again.

August 16: God, Help Me to Be Open to Feedback

Prayer: "Jesus, I can be so sensitive sometimes. Lord, help me to be open to constructive feedback. I want to grow and improve while staying true to myself."

Scripture Reference: "Wise people accept instruction." —Proverbs 12:1

Contemplation: How do you respond to feedback?

Daily Reminder: "Feedback helps me grow."

Engaging Prompt: Ask a trusted friend for feedback on something you're working on.

My Tender Prayer: "God, guide me to practice gratitude for the healing I've experienced. Help me acknowledge the progress I've made. Amen."

Reflection Prompt: Take a long soak or shower and feel your spirit cleansed as well.

August 17: God, Help Me to Reflect on My Journey

Prayer: "Hey God, help me to reflect on my journey and appreciate how far I've come. Each step is part of my authentic path."

Scripture Reference: "I have fought the good fight, I have finished the race, I have kept the faith." —2 Timothy 4:7

Contemplation: What milestones in your journey have shaped your authenticity?

Daily Reminder: "My journey is uniquely mine."

Engaging Prompt: Create a timeline of your life, noting significant moments that contributed to your growth.

My Tender Prayer: "Lord, teach me to welcome change as a sacred part of my healing journey. Help me to release what no longer serves me with grace and to find strength in letting go of the past. Guide me to move forward with an open heart, trusting that each step brings me closer to the wholeness and peace You have planned for me. Amen."

Reflection Prompt: What changes are you resisting? Reflect on how embracing change could facilitate your healing.

August 18: God, Help Me to Cultivate Patience

Prayer: "Jesus, help me to cultivate patience with myself and others. Growth and authenticity take time."

Scripture Reference: "Come to me, all you who are weary and burdened, and I will give you rest. Take my yoke upon you and learn from me, for I am gentle and humble in heart, and you will find rest for your souls." — Matthew 11:28-30

Contemplation: In what areas of your life do you need to practice more patience?

Daily Reminder: "Patience brings peace."

Engaging Prompt: Practice mindfulness today—take a moment to breathe and enjoy the present.

My Tender Prayer: "Dear God, may I celebrate my resilience and strength. Teach me to recognize my ability to rise after setbacks. Amen."

Reflection Prompt: Reflect on a time you demonstrated resilience. How did that experience contribute to your healing?

August 19: God, Help Me to Share My Story

Prayer: "Hey God, I have tried to blend in. I have tried to lay low. I have tried to stay quiet. But I hear your calling, Lord, help me to share my story authentically. I want to inspire others by being open about my journey."

Scripture Reference: "They overcame by the blood of the Lamb and the word of their testimony." —Revelation 12:11

Contemplation: What parts of your story do you feel ready to share?

Daily Reminder: "My story holds power."

Engaging Prompt: Consider sharing your story in a blog, social media post, or with friends.

My Tender Prayer: "God, help me engage in creative expression as a means of healing. May I find freedom in art, writing, or movement. Amen."

Reflection Prompt: Do something surprising today.

August 20: God, Help Me to Stay Grounded

Prayer: "Jesus, help me to stay grounded in my values and beliefs amidst external pressures."

Scripture Reference: "Therefore everyone who hears these words of mine and puts them into practice is like a wise man who built his house on the rock." —Matthew 7:24

Contemplation: What external pressures challenge your authenticity?

Daily Reminder: "I stand firm in my beliefs."

Engaging Prompt: Spend time in nature today, reconnecting with your roots and values.

My Tender Prayer: "Lord, guide me to practice mindfulness as a tool for healing. Help me remain present in each moment. Amen."

Reflection Prompt: After some quiet time, don't you always feel refreshed?

August 21: God, Help Me to Recognize My Worth

Prayer: "Hey God, help me truly see my worth and value as the incredible person You've created me to be. Remind me daily that I am deserving of love, respect, and all the good things this life has to offer. Teach me to stand tall in my truth, to honor myself with the same compassion and care that You show me. Let me embrace my worth unapologetically and walk in the confidence of knowing I am worthy of all the love and joy You have for me. Amen"

Scripture Reference: "You are precious and honored in my sight." —Isaiah 43:4

Contemplation: How do you currently view your worth?

Daily Reminder: "I am worthy, just as I am."

Engaging Prompt: RELAX.

My Tender Prayer: "Heavenly Father, help me embrace self-discovery as a part of healing. Teach me to explore who I am becoming. Amen."

Reflection Prompt: What have you discovered about yourself through prayer? Reflect on the changes you've experienced.

August 22: God, Help Me to Practice Self-Compassion

Prayer: "Jesus, help me to embrace self-compassion and forgive myself for the mistakes of my past. Teach me to release any shame or guilt I've been carrying and replace it with the kindness and understanding I so freely offer others. Show me how to be gentle with myself, to learn and grow from my experiences, and to walk forward with a heart full of grace. Let me love myself the way You love me—unconditionally and without judgment. Amen."

Scripture Reference: "Be kind to one another, tenderhearted, forgiving one another, as God in Christ forgave you." —Ephesians 4:32

Contemplation: How can you be more compassionate towards yourself?

Daily Reminder: "Self-compassion nurtures my soul."

Engaging Prompt: Write a letter of forgiveness to yourself for a past mistake.

My Tender Prayer: "God, May I find hope in the process of understanding myself deeper. Help me visualize the bright future that lies ahead. Amen."

Reflection Prompt: Look at the stars tonight.

August 23: God, Help Me to Embrace Change

Prayer: "Hey God, help me to embrace change with open arms and see it for what it truly is—an opportunity for growth and a deeper connection to my authentic self. Teach me to welcome the shifts in my life, knowing they are leading me to become more of who I'm meant to be. Help me move through the uncertainty with trust and confidence, knowing that with every change, I'm growing into a more powerful, true version of myself. Amen."

Scripture Reference: "And we know that in all things God works for the good of those who love him, who have been called according to his purpose." — Ephesians 4:32

Contemplation: What changes in your life are you resisting?

Daily Reminder: "Change is a part of my journey."

Engaging Prompt: Reflect on a recent change and how it has contributed to your growth.

My Tender Prayer: "Lord, teach me to find peace in solitude. Help me embrace moments of quiet as opportunities for renewal. Amen."

Reflection Prompt: How do you feel about spending time alone? Write about how solitude can support your healing journey.

August 24: God, Help Me to Seek Connection

Prayer: "Jesus, help me to seek genuine connections with others. I want to foster relationships that uplift and inspire me."

Scripture Reference: "Yet you, Lord, are our Father. We are the clay, you are the potter; we are all the work of your hand." — Isaiah 64:8

Contemplation: Who in your life brings out your authentic self?

Daily Reminder: "Connection fuels my spirit."

Engaging Prompt: Plan a gathering or outing with friends to strengthen your connections.

My Tender Prayer: "Dear God, help me cultivate joy in the little things. Teach me to appreciate life's simple pleasures. Amen."

Reflection Prompt: What small joys have you experienced lately? Reflect on how they contribute to your overall well-being.

August 25: God, Help Me to Focus on My Journey

Prayer: "Hey God, as a woman navigating this journey, help me to stop comparing my story to others. I want to embrace my unique path, trusting that the experiences I've had, the choices I make, and the steps I take are all part of Your perfect plan for me. Guide me to celebrate my growth, even when it doesn't look like someone else's. Remind me that I am enough just as I am, with all of my imperfections, strengths, and potential. Help me to honor my journey with grace, patience, and a heart full of trust in You. Amen."

Scripture Reference: "For we are God's handiwork, created in Christ Jesus to do good works." —Ephesians 2:10

Contemplation: What comparisons do you need to let go of?

Daily Reminder: "I honor my unique journey."

Engaging Prompt: Write a letter to yourself, affirming your journey and progress.

My Tender Prayer: "God, help me to trust in the slow, beautiful process of healing. Teach me to savor each step, to embrace my body, my desires, and my growth as I unfold into who I'm meant to be. Let me release the need for instant gratification, and instead, enjoy the journey with confidence, passion, and patience. Guide me to honor my sensuality as part of the healing, knowing that every moment of it is a gift from You. Amen."

Reflection Prompt: How can you pamper your senses today?

August 26: God, Help Me to Trust My Instincts

Prayer: "Jesus, guide me to trust the deep wisdom within me, both my instincts and my faith. Help me to listen to the quiet whispers of my heart, knowing that You've equipped me with everything I need to make wise choices. Strengthen my confidence in following the path You've set before me, and may my decisions reflect both the courage to honor my inner voice and the grace to trust in Your guidance. Amen."

Scripture Reference: "Trust in the Lord with all your heart and lean not on your own understanding." —Proverbs 3:5

Contemplation: When have you ignored your heart in the past?

Daily Reminder: "My faith is a gift."

Engaging Prompt: Spend time in quiet Contemplation, listening to your heart.

My Tender Prayer: "Lord, help me connect with nature as a source of healing and renewal. May I find solace in the world around me. Amen."

Reflection Prompt: What natural settings bring you peace? Write about how spending time in nature supports your healing.

August 27: God, Help Me to Embrace Imperfection

Prayer: "Hey God, help me to embrace my imperfections and understand that they make me who I am."

Scripture Reference: "His strength is made perfect in weakness." —2 Corinthians 12:9

Contemplation: What imperfections have you been struggling to accept?

Daily Reminder: "Imperfection is part of my authenticity."

Engaging Prompt: Celebrate an imperfection of yours that makes you unique.

My Tender Prayer: "Heavenly Father, guide me to seek professional support when needed. Teach me that it's okay to ask for help, whether that's a personal trainer or a physician or a plumber. Amen."

Reflection Prompt: When was the last time you sought help? Reflect on the importance of professional support in your journey.

August 28: God, Help Me to Pursue My Passions

Prayer: "Jesus, help me to pursue my passions wholeheartedly. I want to live a life filled with joy and purpose."

Scripture Reference: "Delight yourself in the Lord, and he will give you the desires of your heart." —Psalm 37:4

Contemplation: What passions have you neglected that you'd like to revisit?

Daily Reminder: "Pursuing my passions fuels my spirit."

Engaging Prompt: Dedicate time this week to engage in a passion or hobby you love.

My Tender Prayer: "God, may I find inspiration in the stories of others who have healed. Help me learn from their journeys. Amen."

Reflection Prompt: Whose healing journey inspires you? Write about what you admire and how it encourages you.

August 29: God, Help Me to Celebrate My Achievements

Prayer: "Hey God, help me to celebrate my achievements, no matter how small. Sometimes simple things are the real treasures. Each step is worth acknowledging."

Scripture Reference: "Rejoice with those who rejoice." —Romans 12:15

Contemplation: What achievements have you overlooked?

Daily Reminder: "Every achievement is a victory."

Engaging Prompt: Write down three achievements you're proud of this month.

My Tender Prayer: "Lord, help me celebrate my unique story. Teach me that it's okay to move at my own pace. Amen."

Reflection Prompt: What makes your story unique?

August 30: God, Help Me to Be Present

Prayer: "Jesus, help me to be present in my life. I want to savor each moment and embrace my journey."

Scripture Reference: "Do not worry about tomorrow, for tomorrow will worry about itself." —Matthew 6:34

Contemplation: What distracts you from being present?

Daily Reminder: "Today is a gift; I will cherish it."

Engaging Prompt: Spend 10 minutes in silence today, focusing on your breath and being present.

My Tender Prayer: "Dear God, as this month ends, thank You for the healing I've experienced. Help me carry this renewal into the next chapter of my life. Amen."

Reflection Prompt: Take yourself out to dinner.

August 31: God, Help Me to Trust in Your Plan

Prayer: "Hey God, as this month comes to a close, help me to surrender my worries and trust wholeheartedly in the plan You have for me. I know that when I live authentically, I align with Your purpose and find true fulfillment. Give me the strength to embrace my true self, knowing that each step I take is part of Your beautiful design for my life. Amen."

Scripture Reference: "For I know the plans I have for you, declares the Lord." —Jeremiah 29:11

Contemplation: How can you continue to live authentically moving in social circles?

Daily Reminder: "I trust in God's perfect plan."

Engaging Prompt: Write down three actionable steps to maintain your authentic self in the coming month.

My Tender Prayer: ""Hey God, as this month of healing comes to a close, help me to fully embrace the lessons and growth I've experienced, especially in embracing my sensuality with confidence and joy. Thank You for awakening a deeper understanding of my body, my desires, and my feminine power. May I carry this renewal forward with playful energy and a heart open to love, pleasure, and grace. Let me celebrate all that I am and continue to walk in the faith of being fully me—beautiful, sensual, and radiant. Amen."

Reflection Prompt: What aspects of your sensuality have you come to appreciate more this month? Reflect on how you can continue to honor and celebrate your body, desires, and feminine energy as you move forward in your journey. How can you integrate more joy, playfulness, and sensuality into your daily life?

September: Rest, Reflection & Reset

September encourages us to slow down and take a breath. As we transition into the fall, we're reminded of the importance of rest and reflection. This month serves as a reminder to pause, recharge, and reset our intentions. It's a time to reflect on our journeys, learn from the past, and prepare our hearts for the seasons ahead. Welcome to September! This month invites us to Rest, Reflect, and Reset. After the journey of authenticity, it's time to take a step back and rejuvenate. Life can be overwhelming, and it's essential to pause, check in with ourselves, and allow our minds and hearts the rest they deserve.

As we embrace the changing season, let's find time for reflection, rediscover our priorities, and set intentions for the coming months. This month is about slowing down, nourishing our spirits, and finding clarity amid chaos.

September 1: God, Help Me to Find Rest

Prayer: "Hey God, today I ask for the gift of rest. Help me to slow down and embrace stillness."

Scripture Reference: "Come to me, all you who are weary and burdened, and I will give you rest." —Matthew 11:28

Contemplation: What areas of your life feel overwhelming right now?

Daily Reminder: "Rest is a necessary part of life."

Engaging Prompt: Schedule a time this week for self-care—be it a cozy night in or a day spent doing what you love.

My Tender Prayer: "Hey God, help me trust in my faith and let it shine through every part of who I am—my body, my spirit, my desires. May I hear Your guiding voice loud and clear, reminding me that I am strong, beautiful, and worthy of all the good things You have for me. Let my faith empower me to walk confidently in my femininity, embrace my body with love, and make choices that reflect the fierce woman You've created me to be. Amen."

Reflection Prompt: What does your faith feel like? Write about a time when you followed your gut feeling.

September 2: God, Help Me to Reflect on My Journey

Prayer: "Jesus, guide me to pause and truly reflect on the path I've walked. Help me to see the strength I've gained, the lessons I've learned, and the growth I've embraced along the way. Teach me to honor how far I've come, with gratitude for every step, every challenge, and every victory. May I move forward with a deep appreciation for my journey and the wisdom it's given me. Amen."

Scripture Reference: "Be still and know that I am God." —Psalm 46:10

Contemplation: What milestones have shaped your journey this year?

Daily Reminder: "Contemplation brings clarity and growth."

Engaging Prompt: Write about a significant moment from the past 30 days and what you learned from it.

My Tender Prayer: "Lord, sharpen my awareness so I can hear the whispers of my heart. Teach me to distinguish between fear and faith. Amen."

Reflection Prompt: How can you differentiate between fear and genuine faith? Reflect on a recent decision where this distinction was important.

September 3: God, Help Me to Release What No Longer Serves Me

Prayer: "Hey God, help me release the burdens I've been carrying—the weight of negative thoughts and past fears that hold me back. Show me how to let go of anything that no longer serves my growth or peace, and make space for healing, joy, and positivity."

Scripture Reference: "Therefore, if anyone is in Christ, the new creation has come: The old has gone, the new is here. —2 Corinthians 5:17

Contemplation: What do you need to release to make room for new beginnings?

Daily Reminder: "Letting go opens space for healing."

Engaging Prompt: Make a list of things you want to let go of this month, then find a peaceful way to release them.

My Tender Prayer: "Heavenly Father, guide me to listen deeply to my inner wisdom. May I honor the insights You provide me. Amen."

Reflection Prompt: Listen to your body.

September 4: God, Help Me to Practice Gratitude

Prayer: "Jesus, help me to open my heart wide in gratitude for all the beauty, love, and blessings in my life. Teach me to savor the moments of sensual pleasure, the quiet joys, and the powerful love that flows through me. Help me appreciate the woman I am—the strength of my body, the depth of my heart, and the light of my spirit. May I embrace every part of myself with love and gratitude, knowing that You've created me to experience life fully and deeply. Amen."

Scripture Reference: "Let us come before him with thanksgiving and extol him with music and song." —Psalm 95:2

Contemplation: Is it easy to be grateful?

Daily Reminder: "Gratitude transforms my perspective."

Engaging Prompt: Write down at least three things you're thankful for today.

My Tender Prayer: "God, help me quiet the noise around me so I can hear Your voice and my own inner guidance. Amen."

Reflection Prompt: What practices help you find stillness? Write about how you can incorporate more quiet time into your life.

September 5: God, Help Me to Seek Peace

Prayer: "Hey God, guide me in seeking peace in my heart and mind. I want to feel centered amidst life's chaos."

Scripture Reference: "Peace I leave with you; my peace I give you." —John 14:27

Contemplation: What brings you a sense of peace?

Daily Reminder: "Peace is a state of mind I can cultivate."

Engaging Prompt: Spend 10 minutes in silence or meditation today, focusing on your breath and finding inner peace.

My Tender Prayer: "Lord, may I have the courage to act on my faith, even when it feels uncomfortable. Help me trust that You are with me. Amen."

Reflection Prompt: When has following your faith led you to a positive outcome? Reflect on that experience and how it felt.

September 6: God, Help Me to Prioritize Self-Care

Prayer: "Jesus, help me to see the profound importance of self-care in my life. Teach me to honor my body, mind, and spirit as sacred gifts from You. May I prioritize rest, nourishment, and moments of peace, knowing that caring for myself allows me to love and serve others better. Help me to embrace self-care not as selfishness, but as a necessary act of self-respect and grace. Guide me to find balance, listen to my needs, and create space for renewal, so that I can live with strength, joy, and purpose. Amen."

Scripture Reference: "Dear friend, I pray that you may enjoy good health and that all may go well with you." —3 John 12

Contemplation: What self-care practices do you need to incorporate into your routine?

Daily Reminder: "Self-care is not selfish; it's essential."

Engaging Prompt: Plan a self-care day—what activities will you include?

My Tender Prayer: "Dear God, I know I've been through some wild stuff, but I'm ready to let You turn it all into wisdom. Help me embrace the lessons in my experiences, no matter how messy or beautiful they've been. I want to grow stronger and smarter with every moment, and trust You've been guiding me even when I didn't realize it. Teach me to see every challenge as a chance to get closer to who I'm meant to be, and to embrace that power with grace. Amen."

Reflection Prompt: How can I give grace to others in ways that make my life easier or give a sense of calm.

September 7: God, Help Me to Listen to My Body

Prayer: "Hey God, help me to listen to my body and understand its needs. I want to honor it through rest and nourishment."

Scripture Reference: "Do you not know that you are God's temple and that God's Spirit dwells in you?" —1 Corinthians 3:16

Contemplation: What signals is your body sending you?

Daily Reminder: "My body deserves love and care."

Engaging Prompt: Take a moment to assess your body's needs—do you need more sleep, better nutrition, or relaxation?

My Tender Prayer: "God, may I connect with my inner child and the wisdom it holds. Teach me to honor my feelings and instincts. Amen."

Reflection Prompt: What does your inner child want to tell you? Write a letter to your younger self, acknowledging their wisdom.

September 8: God, Help Me to Create a Vision for My Future

Prayer: "Jesus, help me to plan for my future with clarity and purpose. I want to align my goals with your plans."

Scripture Reference: "Where there is no vision, the people perish." —Proverbs 29:18

Contemplation: What dreams and goals are you passionate about pursuing?

Daily Reminder: "Creating a vision empowers my journey."

Engaging Prompt: Spend time crafting a goal collage that reflects your aspirations and intentions for the coming months.

My Tender Prayer: "Lord, help me embrace uncertainty as a part of my journey. May I find strength in trusting my faith despite not knowing the outcome. Amen."

Reflection Prompt: How do you feel about uncertainty? Reflect on how trusting your faith can provide comfort during uncertain times.

September 9: God, Help Me to Journal My Thoughts

Prayer: "Hey God, I come to You with a heart open to understanding myself more deeply. Please guide me as I use journaling as a tool for reflection. Help me to create space in my heart and mind where I can pour out my thoughts, my feelings, and the things that weigh heavy on me. Teach me how to use this process not just as a way to vent, but as a path to clarity, healing, and self-awareness. May the words I write lead me to a deeper connection with You, allowing me to better understand my own heart and how it aligns with Your will. Help me to listen to the wisdom within me as I write, and to gain insight into the lessons You are teaching me through each reflection. Amen."

Scripture Reference: "Write the concept; make it plain on tablets." —Habakkuk 2:2

Contemplation: How does journaling help you process your emotions?

Daily Reminder: "Writing brings clarity and healing."

Engaging Prompt: Take your journaling to the next level.

My Tender Prayer: "Heavenly Father, help me to surround myself with people who encourage my faith and inner wisdom. Amen."

Reflection Prompt: What were your dreams as a child?

September 10: God, Help Me to Embrace Solitude

Prayer: "Jesus, help me to embrace solitude as a time for personal growth and reflection. I want to find strength in being alone."

Scripture Reference: "But Jesus often withdrew to lonely places and prayed." —Luke 5:16

Contemplation: What do you enjoy doing in your alone time?

Daily Reminder: "Solitude nurtures my spirit."

Engaging Prompt: Plan a quiet evening alone to unwind and engage in an activity you love.

My Tender Prayer: "God, May I practice self-reflection and gain clarity about my feelings and desires. Teach me to listen to my heart. Amen."

Reflection Prompt: What do you truly desire in this moment? Reflect on your heart's yearnings and how you can honor them.

September 11: God, Help Me to Foster Connection

Prayer: "Hey God, I'm ready to build the kind of connections that actually light me up. Help me to attract people who vibe with my soul, people who uplift, inspire, and challenge me to grow. I want relationships that are real, that nourish my heart and help me become the best version of myself. Give me the wisdom to set boundaries where needed and the courage to show up authentically. May I surround myself with people who see me for who I am—fierce, beautiful, and worthy of deep, meaningful connections. Amen."

Scripture Reference: "Every day they continued to meet together in the temple courts. They broke bread in their homes and ate together with glad and sincere hearts." —Acts 2:46-47

Contemplation: Who do you feel most connected to in your life?

Daily Reminder: "Connection is essential for my well-being."

Engaging Prompt: Reach out to someone you care about and schedule time to catch up.

My Tender Prayer: "Lord, help me recognize synchronicities in my life as signs of Your guidance. May I remain open to the messages You send me. Amen."

Reflection Prompt: Have you experienced any coincidences that felt significant? Write about how they might be guiding you.

September 12: God, Help Me to Cultivate Mindfulness

Prayer: "Jesus, help me to stay grounded and in the moment, even when life gets busy or distracting. I want to fully experience each day, with all of my senses alive and engaged. Teach me to embrace mindfulness in everything I do, whether it's feeling the warmth of the sun on my skin, savoring every bite of food, or just being present with the people I care about. Help me to slow down and appreciate the beauty of each moment, so I can live with intention and purpose. Let me feel alive in every step I take. Amen."

Scripture Reference: "Be still and know that I am God." —Psalm 46:10

Contemplation: How can you practice mindfulness today?

Daily Reminder: "Mindfulness brings clarity and peace."

Engaging Prompt: Choose an activity today and commit to being fully present during it—whether it's eating, walking, or conversing.

My Tender Prayer: "Dear God, teach me to find peace within myself. May I discover the wisdom that resides in my heart. Amen."

Reflection Prompt: Even a walk in the park can be an act of mindfulness.

September 13: God, Help Me to Be Open to Change

Prayer: "Hey God, I know change can be scary, but I'm ready to embrace it with an open heart. Help me to release the old and welcome the new, trusting that You've got something amazing ahead. I want to stay open to the opportunities You're placing before me, even when they challenge me to step out of my comfort zone. Teach me to see change not as a loss, but as a chance for growth, transformation, and deeper connection with You. I'm ready for what's next—bring it on! Amen."

Scripture Reference: "Therefore, if anyone is in Christ, the new creation has come: The old has gone, the new is here!" —2 Corinthians 5:17

Contemplation: What changes are you resisting, and how might they benefit you?

Daily Reminder: "Change is a natural part of life."

Engaging Prompt: Think about a recent change in your life—whether it's a shift in perspective, a new opportunity, or a surprising twist. How has it shaken things up for you? Write about how this change has affected you, and what it's taught you about yourself and your desires.

My Tender Prayer: "God, help me to stay present in every moment, fully embracing the sensations, the beauty, and the energy that each one brings. Guide me to trust my intuition and my faith as I make decisions that honor the desires of my body, heart, and spirit. May I feel Your presence in every breath, every touch, and every step, knowing that You've created me to live with passion and purpose. Amen."

Reflection Prompt: Try to pay attention to everything around you for 60 seconds.

September 14: God, Help Me to Be Compassionate Towards Others

Prayer: "Jesus, help me to be compassionate towards others, recognizing that everyone is on their own journey."

Scripture Reference: "Be kind and compassionate to one another, forgiving each other, just as in Christ God forgave you." —Ephesians 4:32

Contemplation: How can you show compassion to someone in your life?

Daily Reminder: "Compassion strengthens my connections."

Engaging Prompt: Perform a small act of kindness for someone this week—whether it's a compliment, helping hand, or listening ear.

My Tender Prayer: "Lord, help me to journal my thoughts and feelings as a way to clarify my inner voice. May my writing reveal the wisdom I seek. Amen."

Reflection Prompt: Write a postcard to yourself as if you sent it from somewhere you'd like to travel one day.

September 15: God, Help Me to Evaluate My Goals

Prayer: "Hey God, help me to evaluate my goals and determine which ones align with my authentic self."

Scripture Reference: "Commit to the Lord whatever you do, and he will establish your plans." —Proverbs 16:3

Contemplation: Which of your goals still resonate with you?

Daily Reminder: "Evaluating my goals helps me stay true to myself."

Engaging Prompt: Review your current goals and write down which ones you want to keep, adjust, or let go of.

My Tender Prayer: "Heavenly Father, teach me to seek guidance from within before looking outward. Help me trust my inner compass. Amen."

Reflection Prompt: When was the last time you sought advice from others instead of trusting yourself? Reflect on how you can shift this pattern.

September 16: God, Help Me to Seek Balance

Prayer: "Jesus, guide me in seeking balance in my life. I want to nurture all areas—mind, body, and spirit."

Scripture Reference: "A heart at peace gives life to the body." —Proverbs 14:30

Contemplation: How balanced do you feel in your daily life?

Daily Reminder: "Balance fosters harmony."

Engaging Prompt: Assess your daily routines and make adjustments to create more balance in your life.

My Tender Prayer: "God, may I cultivate a sense of curiosity about my thoughts and feelings. Teach me to explore without judgment. Amen."

Reflection Prompt: What makes you curious?

September 17: God, Help Me to Embrace Vulnerability

Prayer: "Hey God, help me to embrace vulnerability, even when it feels like a scary movie plot. I want to be open to deeper connections, richer experiences, and real, raw moments with others. Show me that being vulnerable isn't weakness; it's where the magic happens. Help me lean into the unknown with courage and an open heart, ready to let go and truly experience the beauty of connection. Amen."

Scripture Reference: "My grace is sufficient for you, for my power is made perfect in weakness." —2 Corinthians 12:9

Contemplation: What might the birds be singing about?

Daily Reminder: "Vulnerability is a strength."

Engaging Prompt: Share something personal with someone you trust—this can deepen your relationship and foster connection.

My Tender Prayer: "God, may I cultivate a sense of curiosity about my thoughts and feelings. Teach me to explore without judgment. Amen."

Reflection Prompt: Sing in the shower, how does that feel?

September 18: God, Help Me to Set Boundaries

Prayer: "Lord, guide me in understanding the power and necessity of setting healthy boundaries in my life. Teach me that protecting my peace and energy isn't selfish—it's essential for my well-being. Help me to know when to say no, when to step back, and when to stand firm, all while remaining compassionate and kind. Show me that establishing boundaries is an act of self-respect and love, and let me honor myself in every relationship. Amen."

Scripture Reference: "The prudent see danger and take refuge, but the simple keep going and pay the penalty." —Proverbs 22:3

Contemplation: What boundaries do you need to establish or reinforce?

Daily Reminder: "Setting boundaries is an act of self-care."

Engaging Prompt: Identify one boundary you'd like to set and outline steps to communicate it effectively.

My Tender Prayer: "Dear God, may I learn to accept the wisdom of my body. Help me listen to its signals and honor its needs. Amen."

Reflection Prompt: How does your body communicate its needs to you? Reflect on a recent time when you followed your body's signals.

September 19: God, Help Me to Cultivate a Positive Mindset

Prayer: "Hey God, help me to cultivate a positive mindset. I want to focus on the good in my life and see challenges as opportunities."

Scripture Reference: "Finally, brothers and sisters, whatever is true, whatever is noble, whatever is right, whatever is pure, whatever is lovely, whatever is admirable—if anything is excellent or praiseworthy—think about such things." —Philippians 4:8

Contemplation: How can you shift your perspective on a current challenge?

Daily Reminder: "A positive mindset fuels my spirit."

Engaging Prompt: Write down three positive ways to look at situations in your life.

My Tender Prayer: "God, open my heart to the wisdom of those around me, allowing their words to nourish my spirit. And my reflection on their meaning to deepen my understanding of who I am as a woman, embracing my sensuality and femininity while finding meaning in my experiences. Amen."

Reflection Prompt: How do you feel about receiving feedback? Write about how you can reframe feedback as a tool for growth.

September 20: God, Help Me to Take a Break from Social Media

Prayer: "Jesus, help me to take a break from social media (if even just for an hour or two) and focus on my own journey without comparison."

Scripture Reference: "Set your minds on things that are above, not on things that are on earth." —Colossians 3:2

Contemplation: How does social media impact your views of your own life?

Daily Reminder: "Focusing on myself brings clarity."

Engaging Prompt: Consider a social media detox this week. What will you do with the time you free up?

My Tender Prayer: "Lord, help me recognize the patterns in my life that provide insight into my life. May I learn from these experiences. Amen."

Reflection Prompt: What recurring patterns do you notice in your decisions? Reflect on how they might inform your faith moving forward.

September 21: God, Help Me to Seek Your Guidance

Prayer: " Show me how to honor my sensuality and femininity while chasing after the goals You've planted in my heart. Guide me to move through life with purpose, trust, and that undeniable sparkle, knowing I'm walking in Your plan every step of the way. Amen."

Scripture Reference: "Trust in the Lord with all your heart and lean not on your own understanding; in all your ways submit to him, and he will make your paths straight." —Proverbs 3:5-6

Contemplation: What areas of your life need God's guidance?

Daily Reminder: "God's wisdom lights my path."

Engaging Prompt: Spend time in prayer, asking God for clarity on your current situation.

My Tender Prayer: "Heavenly Father, may I approach life with a sense of wonder and exploration. Teach me to see opportunities for growth in every experience. Amen."

Reflection Prompt: What excites you about exploring new ideas? Write about a new interest or passion you want to pursue.

September 22: God, Help Me to Reflect on My Relationships

Prayer: "Jesus, help me to reflect on my relationships and evaluate which ones uplift my spirit."

Scripture Reference: "Above all, love each other deeply, because love covers over a multitude of sins." —1 Peter 4:8

Contemplation: Which relationships nourish your soul?

Daily Reminder: "Healthy relationships enrich my life."

Engaging Prompt: Reach out to someone who brings positivity into your life and express your appreciation for them.

My Tender Prayer: "God, may I find strength in community, learning from others' experiences while trusting my own journey. Amen."

Reflection Prompt: Laughter alone vs with friends.

September 23: God, Help Me to Explore New Opportunities

Prayer: "God, show me how to honor my sensuality and femininity as I pursue the friendships and opportunities You've placed in my path. Help me to build meaningful connections that uplift and inspire, while staying true to the goals You've planted deep in my heart. Guide me to move with purpose, grace, and that spark of confidence that comes from trusting Your plan. Let me embrace every opportunity, knowing that each one is part of the beautiful journey You've designed for me. Amen."

Scripture Reference: "The steps of a good man are ordered by the Lord, and He delights in his way." —Psalm 37:23

Contemplation: What new opportunities are you excited to pursue?

Daily Reminder: "Exploring new opportunities expands my horizons."

Engaging Prompt: Research a new hobby, class, or interest you've been considering and take the first step toward exploring it.

My Tender Prayer: "Lord, help me practice self-acceptance as I navigate my faith. Teach me to honor my unique path and choices. Amen."

Reflection Prompt: What aspects of yourself do you struggle to accept? Write about how embracing these parts can enhance your faith.

September 24: God, Help Me to Create a Reset Plan

Prayer: "Jesus, help me hit the reset button and create a plan that actually reflects what I care about and where I want to go. I know it won't be perfect, and things might get messy, but help me to stay real and stay focused on what matters. Guide me through the chaos, so I can align my life with my values and goals—without stressing over every little detail. Let me be bold, a little messy, but always moving forward. Amen."

Scripture Reference: "Trust in the Lord with all your heart and lean not on your own understanding; in all your ways submit to Him, and He will make your paths straight." —Proverbs 3:5-6

Contemplation: What aspects of your life need a reset?

Daily Reminder: "Resetting my life brings clarity and focus."

Engaging Prompt: Outline a simple plan for the next month, including personal, professional, and spiritual goals.

My Tender Prayer: "Hey God, thanks for all the wisdom I've picked up along the way—even the stuff I didn't expect. Help me take these lessons, no matter how messy or wild they were, and use them to level up in the present and future. Show me how to turn my past into power, so I can keep moving forward smarter, stronger, and a whole lot more fabulous. Let me own this journey with confidence and a good laugh along the way. Amen."

Reflection Prompt: Take a long walk and feel the weather.

September 25: God, Help Me to Celebrate My Growth

Prayer: "Hey God, I'm here, and I'm ready to give myself some credit. Help me to celebrate how far I've come, even when the road's been messy or complicated. Every step I've taken, every mistake I've learned from, it's all part of the bigger picture You're painting for me. I want to embrace my journey without shame, knowing that my past doesn't define me. You've been with me through it all, and now I'm ready to keep growing, keep evolving, and keep living boldly, with grace and love for myself. Amen."

Scripture Reference: "Rejoice with those who rejoice." —Romans 12:15

Contemplation: Butterflies, birds, they don't have to understand the wind.

Daily Reminder: "Celebrating growth fuels my journey."

Engaging Prompt: Share your achievements with someone who supports you—celebrate together!

My Tender Prayer: "God, guide me as I explore and embrace the woman I am becoming. Help me to trust the process of revealing my authentic self, with all my beauty, desires, and power. Teach me to see my journey as one of deep self-love and faith, where I honor every part of me—body, mind, and spirit."

Reflection Prompt: sleep in sometime this week.

September 26: God, Help Me to Welcome New Beginnings

Prayer: "Jesus, help me to welcome every new beginning with an open heart and a fearless vibe. I'm ready to embrace whatever's next, knowing it's part of my bigger journey. Guide me to move forward with excitement and trust, even when the unknown feels a little intimidating. Let me step into what's to come with confidence, grace, and that bold, adventurous spirit."

Scripture Reference: "Forget the former things; do not dwell on the past. See, I am doing a new thing!" —Isaiah 43:18-19

Contemplation: What new beginnings are on the horizon for you?

Daily Reminder: "New beginnings bring fresh opportunities."

Engaging Prompt: Write about a new beginning you're excited about and how you plan to embrace it.

My Tender Prayer: "Lord, help me create habits that connect me to my faith as well as my desires. May these practices ground me and enhance my inner wisdom. Amen."

Reflection Prompt: Look out a window and wait until something that catches your attention.

September 27: God, Help Me to Prioritize Rest in My Life

Prayer: "Hey God, help me to actually take a break and prioritize rest. I know I need to honor my body and spirit, so show me how to slow down without feeling guilty. Help me find that sweet spot of balance—where I'm recharged, refreshed, and ready to take on the world. Let me rest with purpose, so I can show up strong and fully me. Amen."

Scripture Reference: "Six days you shall labor and do all your work, but the seventh day is a Sabbath to the Lord your God." —Exodus 20:9-10

Contemplation: How can you incorporate more rest into your routine?

Daily Reminder: "Rest is essential for my well-being."

Engaging Prompt: Plan a mini retreat day for yourself—how will you recharge?

My Tender Prayer: "Heavenly Father, may I remain open to receiving guidance from unexpected sources. Teach me to embrace the unknown. Amen."

Reflection Prompt: Take an alternative route today.

September 28: God, Help Me to Appreciate the Present Moment

Prayer: "Jesus, help me to stop stressing over the future and let go of the past. Help me to really appreciate the present, even when it's messy and chaotic. Show me how to find joy in the now, even in the little, random moments that make life so interesting. Let me laugh, breathe, and just *be* in the here and now. Amen."

Scripture Reference: "Do not worry about tomorrow, for tomorrow will worry about itself." —Matthew 6:34

Contemplation: What keeps you from being present?

Daily Reminder: "Today is a gift; I will cherish it."

Engaging Prompt: Practice mindfulness today—take a walk, savor your food, or simply enjoy silence.

My Tender Prayer: "God, help me find balance between listening to my faith and seeking knowledge from others. May I integrate both in my decision-making. Amen."

Reflection Prompt: Listen to the sounds out the window.

September 29: God, Help Me to Reassess My Values

Prayer: "Hey God, guide me as I reassess my values and ensure my life aligns with what truly matters."

Scripture Reference: "For where your treasure is, there your heart will be also." —Matthew 6:21

Contemplation: What values guide your decisions and actions?

Daily Reminder: "Aligning with my values brings fulfillment."

Engaging Prompt: Write down your top five values and evaluate how they are reflected in your life.

My Tender Prayer: "Lord, help me to see my dreams and desires with crystal-clear vision. Ignite that fire in me, so I can visualize exactly where I'm headed. I know You've got a plan for me, and I trust that my faith will be the fuel to get me there. Guide me as I step into my power, knowing that every dream I have is valid, and I deserve to see them come true. May I move boldly toward my goals, with confidence and passion."

Reflection Prompt: What are the dreams and goals you're feeling called to? Write about how your faith can light the way as you move toward them.

September 30: God, Help Me to Trust the Journey

Prayer: "Jesus, help me to trust the journey, knowing that each step is part of your greater plan for my life."

Scripture Reference: "For I know the plans I have for you, declares the Lord." —Jeremiah 29:11

Contemplation: How can you cultivate trust in your journey moving forward?

Daily Reminder: "I trust in God's perfect timing."

Engaging Prompt: Talk to a friend about your goals.

My Tender Prayer: "Hey God, thank You for the strength You've given me to rise above my past. Even when I've wandered and made choices that didn't always align with my true self, I trust that You've been there, guiding me through it all. Help me to embrace my sensuality, my desires, and the fullness of who I am, knowing that You've never left my side. Teach me to trust Your wisdom and faith, and to lean into that trust with confidence. I'm ready to walk forward, fully embracing my beautiful, bold self. Amen."

Reflection Prompt: Reflect on your journey with faith this month. What have you learned about trusting your inner voice?

Seasonal Message for October, November, and Decemb

As the year begins to finishes up, we enter a sacred space of reflection, resilience, and renewal. The last three months are often filled with introspection as we acknowledge our struggles and victories alike. Here, we will focus on the themes of Fierce Faith in Tough Times, Gratitude, and Redemption and Growth.

October: Fierce Faith in Tough Times

This month challenges us to hold fast to our faith, even when the storms of life threaten to overwhelm us. Tough times can feel isolating, but through prayer and community, we find strength in vulnerability and courage in uncertainty. Our fierce faith can become a beacon of hope, reminding us that we are never alone. We'll explore how to lean into our beliefs and trust God's plan, even when it feels hard to see the light at the end of the tunnel.

November: Gratitude & Grace

As we step into November, we celebrate the power of gratitude in our lives. Gratitude opens our hearts and minds to recognize the blessings that often go unnoticed. This month encourages us to cultivate a habit of thankfulness, shifting our focus from what we lack to what we have. By doing so, we also create space for God's grace to bring us closer to our goals in our lives. We will reflect on the people, experiences, and lessons we cherish, acknowledging that each moment shapes who we are and where we are headed.

December: Redemption & Growth

December invites us to embrace the themes of redemption and growth, marking the year's end with a sense of purpose and renewal. It's a time for reflection, recognizing how far we've come, and the lessons learned along the way. In this sacred season, we are reminded that our past does not define us; instead, it can be a pathway to growth and transformation. As we prepare for a new year, we'll focus on how to carry the lessons into our next chapter, affirming that every ending can spark a new beginning.

October: Fierce Faith in Tough Times

October calls us to stand firm in our faith, even when life's storms feel overwhelming. Hard seasons can feel lonely, but through prayer and community, we discover strength in vulnerability and courage amidst the unknown. This month reminds us that fierce faith is a light that guides us, offering hope and assurance that God is always with us. Together, we'll learn how to lean deeper into our beliefs and trust in His plan, even when the path ahead feels uncertain.

October 1: God, Help Me Stand Firm in My Faith

Prayer: "Hey God, as we step into October, I'm asking for some divine backbone! Life's thrown a few curveballs, and I need help standing firm in my faith, even when things feel like they're crumbling around me. Remind me that your love is a rock that I can lean on."

Scripture Reference: "Be strong and take heart, all you who hope in the Lord." —Psalm 31:24

Contemplation: What challenges are testing your faith right now? How can you draw on your relationship with God to navigate these storms?

Daily Reminder: "My faith is my foundation; it keeps me steady when the world spins around me."

Engaging Prompt: Write down one significant challenge you're facing. Reflect on how your faith has been a source of strength in the past and how you can apply those lessons to your current situation.

My Tender Prayer: "Dear God, grant me the courage to be vulnerable. Help me see my softness as a strength and a reflection of Your love. Amen."

Reflection Prompt: What does vulnerability mean to you? Write about a time when being vulnerable led to a positive outcome.

October 2: God, Help Me to See Your Hand in My Life

Prayer: "Jesus, open my eyes and heart to recognize how you're working in my life, especially when things feel tough. I sometimes get so caught up in my problems that I forget to look for your miracles in the mess."

Scripture Reference: "And we know that in all things God works for the good of those who love him." —Romans 8:28

Contemplation: How can you recognize God's presence in your struggles? Think back to a time when something difficult turned out to be a blessing in disguise.

Daily Reminder: "Even in my struggles, God is weaving a beautiful tapestry of my life."

Engaging Prompt: List three moments from your past where you can clearly see God's hand at work. How did these moments shape your faith?

My Tender Prayer: "Lord, help me embrace my emotions without fear. May I express them with love and honesty, knowing they are valid. Amen."

Reflection Prompt: Reflect on an emotion you've been avoiding. What would it feel like to express it openly today?

October 3: God, Help Me to Trust Your Plan

Prayer: "Hey God, it's hard sometimes, but I know I need to trust your plan, even when my navigation system seems to be rerouting constantly. Help me to embrace the unknown and have faith that you're guiding me on a path that's better than I can imagine."

Scripture Reference: "For I am about to do something new. See, I have already begun! Do you not see it?" —Isaiah 43:19

Contemplation: What fears or anxieties do you need to surrender to God today? What's holding you back from fully trusting in His plan?

Daily Reminder: "I release my fears to God; His plans are greater than my own."

Engaging Prompt: Write about a time when you saw God's plan unfold in a way you never expected. What did you learn about trust through that experience?

My Tender Prayer: "Heavenly Father, teach me to show kindness to myself, especially during difficult moments. May I treat myself with love and compassion. Amen."

Reflection Prompt: How do you typically respond to yourself during hard times? Write about ways you can practice self-kindness.

October 4: God, Help Me to Find Peace in Chaos

Prayer: "Jesus, with all the chaos in my life, I'm craving peace that only you can provide. Help me to center myself in you and remember that no storm lasts forever."

Scripture Reference: "Do not be anxious about anything, but in every situation, by prayer and petition, with thanksgiving, present your requests to God." —Philippians 4:6

Contemplation: Where do you need God's peace the most in your life right now? How can you cultivate that peace through prayer and mindfulness?

Daily Reminder: "Peace is a choice, and I choose to seek it daily."

Engaging Prompt: Find peace in doing the ordinary.

My Tender Prayer: "God, help me embrace my true strength by leaning into my vulnerability. Teach me that there is power in showing up as my authentic, unfiltered self—body, heart, and soul. May I find freedom in expressing all that I am, and may I never shrink back from my desires, my beauty, or my truth. Help me stand confidently in the fullness of who You've created me to be, knowing that I am both powerful and precious in Your eyes. Amen."

Reflection Prompt: Think about a time when you allowed yourself to be fully vulnerable—whether emotionally, physically, or spiritually. How did it feel to shed the layers and show your true self? Write about how embracing that vulnerability empowered you and shifted your sense of strength and confidence.

October 5: God, Help Me to Lean on My Community

Prayer: "Hey God, remind me of the importance of community during tough times. It's so easy to feel alone in my struggles, but I know that you've surrounded me with people who care. Show me how to reach out and ask for support."

Scripture Reference: "Two are better than one, because they have a good return for their labor." —Ecclesiastes 4:9

Contemplation: Who in your life provides support during difficult moments? How can you lean on them more this month?

Daily Reminder: "I am surrounded by love and support; I am not alone."

Engaging Prompt: Reach out to a friend or family member or even a stranger today. Share how you're feeling and ask how they're doing. Let's build those connections!

My Tender Prayer: "Lord, guide me in building connections that are rooted in vulnerability and trust. Help me to create a safe space where I can truly open up, allowing others to do the same. Let these connections be real, raw, and deeply nurturing—filled with compassion and understanding. Teach me to embrace the beauty of sharing, knowing that true intimacy begins with honest, heartfelt communication. Amen."

Reflection Prompt: Think of someone you trust. How can you deepen your connection with them through vulnerability?

October 6: God, Help Me to Turn My Worries into Prayers

Prayer: "Jesus, teach me to turn my worries into prayers. I often let my mind spiral, but I know that surrendering my concerns to you will lighten my load. Help me remember that worry doesn't change the outcome, but prayer does."

Scripture Reference: "Cast all your anxiety on him because he cares for you." —1 Peter 5:7

Contemplation: What worries are weighing you down? How can turning those worries into prayers transform your mindset?

Daily Reminder: "I choose to cast my worries on God and embrace His peace."

Engaging Prompt: Write a letter to God today, pouring out your worries. Once you're done, find a way to symbolically release them—like tearing up the letter.

My Tender Prayer: "Dear God, teach me to let go of perfectionism. May I embrace my imperfections as part of my unique beauty. Amen."

Reflection Prompt: What areas of your life do you feel pressured to be perfect? Reflect on how embracing imperfection can free you.

October 7: God, Help Me to Remember My Strength

Prayer: "Hey God, as I navigate tough times, remind me of the strength you've given me. Sometimes I forget just how resilient I am! Let my challenges reveal my courage, not diminish it."

Scripture Reference: "I can do all this through him who gives me strength." —Philippians 4:13

Contemplation: What past challenges have shown you just how strong you are? How can these memories empower you today?

Daily Reminder: "My strength comes from God, and I am capable of overcoming anything."

Engaging Prompt: List three challenges you've overcome in your life. Celebrate your resilience! How can you draw on these experiences when facing current struggles?

My Tender Prayer: "God, help me practice vulnerability in my relationships. May I share my thoughts and feelings openly with those I love. Amen."

Reflection Prompt: Who in your life would you like to be more vulnerable with? Write about what you'd like to share.

October 8: God, Help Me to Seek Joy in the Little Things

Prayer: "Jesus, help me to find joy in the little things, especially during tough times. It's easy to overlook the small blessings when I'm overwhelmed, but I know they're all around me. Teach me to embrace them!"

Scripture Reference: "Delight yourself in the Lord, and he will give you the desires of your heart." —Psalm 37:4

Contemplation: What small joys are present in your life today? How can you intentionally seek out moments of happiness?

Daily Reminder: "Joy can be found in the ordinary, and I will choose to see it!"

Engaging Prompt: Take a moment today to appreciate something small—like a warm cup of coffee or a favorite song. Write about the experience and how it brought you joy.

My Tender Prayer: "Lord, help me to create a nurturing environment where peace is welcomed. May I encourage others to share their truths. Amen."

Reflection Prompt: How can you foster an atmosphere of openness in your relationships? List three ways you can encourage honesty in others.

October 9: God, Help Me to Speak Life into My Situation

Prayer: "Hey God, help me learn to speak life into my situation rather than dwelling on negativity. My words have power, and I want to use them to uplift myself and those around me."

Scripture Reference: "The tongue has the power of life and death, and those who love it will eat its fruit." —Proverbs 18:21

Contemplation: How can your words shift your perspective today? What phrases can you eliminate from your vocabulary?

Daily Reminder: "It is easy to say something kind."

Engaging Prompt: Tell someone they inspire you today.

My Tender Prayer: "Heavenly Father, may I be gentle with myself as I navigate each day. Help me to honor my feelings without judgment. Amen."

Reflection Prompt: How do you typically respond to your own needs? Reflect on how you can shift this response to one of compassion.

October 10: God, Help Me to Stay Grounded in Faith

Prayer: "Jesus, as the world swirls around me, help me stay grounded in my faith. When everything feels chaotic, I want to remember that my foundation is in you. Teach me to remain steadfast."

Scripture Reference: "Therefore, my dear brothers and sisters, stand firm. Let nothing move you." —1 Corinthians 15:58

Contemplation: What practices keep you grounded in your faith? How can you reinforce these in your daily life?

Daily Reminder: "Staying grounded in faith gives me strength to face the storms."

Engaging Prompt: Identify one spiritual practice you'll commit to this month—whether it's prayer, journaling, or scripture reading. Set a goal to do it regularly and note your experiences.

My Tender Prayer: "God, teach me that being sensual or vulnerable doesn't make me weak. May I find strength in sharing my heart with others. Amen."

Reflection Prompt: When have you admired someone for their vulnerability? What qualities did they exhibit that inspired you?

October 11: God, Help Me to Release Control

Prayer: "Hey God, I'm realizing that I can't control everything—and that's okay! Help me to surrender my need for control and trust in your divine timing. I want to feel the freedom that comes with letting go."

Scripture Reference: "Be still, and know that I am God." —Psalm 46:10

Contemplation: What areas of your life are you trying to control? How can you practice releasing that control?

Daily Reminder: "I trust in God's perfect timing; I will let go of what I cannot change."

Engaging Prompt: What are things that don't really matter that are eating up your time?

My Tender Prayer: "Lord, may I learn to forgive myself for past mistakes and wild nights. Help me embrace my journey with kindness and understanding. Amen."

Reflection Prompt: What do you need to forgive yourself for? Write about how releasing this burden can free you.

October 12: God, Help Me to Find Courage in Uncertainty

Prayer: "Jesus, grant me the courage to move forward, even when the future feels uncertain. Help me remember that your plans for me are good, and you're with me every step of the way."

Scripture Reference: "Have I not commanded you? Be strong and courageous. Do not be afraid; do not be discouraged, for the Lord your God will be with you wherever you go." —Joshua 1:9

Contemplation: What uncertainties are challenging you right now? How can you find courage in your faith amidst these unknowns?

Daily Reminder: "Courage fuels my journey; I will not let fear hold me back."

Engaging Prompt: List three courageous steps you can take this week, even if they feel small. What would you gain from taking these steps?

My Tender Prayer: "Dear God, help me embrace my feelings of sadness or pain without shame. Teach me to see them as part of my growth. Amen."

Reflection Prompt: You are a song.

October 13: God, Help Me to Surrender My Burdens

Prayer: "Hey God, I'm tired of carrying my burdens alone. Help me to surrender them to you. I know you're big enough to handle everything I'm facing, and I want to feel the relief of giving it all to you."

Scripture Reference: "Come to me, all you who are weary and burdened, and I will give you rest." —Matthew 11:28

Contemplation: What burdens do you need to hand over to God? How does it feel to consider releasing them?

Daily Reminder: "Surrender brings peace; I will not carry these weights alone."

Engaging Prompt: Rage a little sometimes.

My Tender Prayer: "God, grant me the courage to share my story. May I inspire others through my journey and my vulnerability. Amen."

Reflection Prompt: What part of your story feels significant to share? Write about how sharing this might impact others.

October 14: God, Help Me to Trust in Your Promises

Prayer: "Jesus, I need your help to trust in your promises, even when things get tough. Remind me that your word is true, and your love is constant, even in uncertainty."

Scripture Reference: "Every promise of God is 'yes' in Christ." —2 Corinthians 1:20

Contemplation: What promises from God do you need to hold onto today? How can these promises anchor you amidst the storms?

Daily Reminder: "God's promises are my anchor; they hold me steady."

Engaging Prompt: Choose a promise from scripture that resonates with you. Write it down and meditate on it throughout the day. How does it change your perspective?

My Tender Prayer: "Lord, may I find beauty in my softness. Help me appreciate the gentle aspects of my personality as gifts. Amen."

Reflection Prompt: What qualities do you consider to be soft or gentle within yourself? Write about how they contribute to your strength.

October 15: God, Help Me to Remember I'm Not Alone

Prayer: "Hey God, remind me that I'm never alone in my struggles. Your presence is my comfort, and I'm grateful for the people you've placed in my life to support me."

Scripture Reference: "I will never leave you nor forsake you." —Hebrews 13:5

Contemplation: Who can you reach out to when you feel alone? How can you remind yourself of God's constant presence?

Daily Reminder: "I am surrounded by love and support; I am not alone."

Engaging Prompt: Text or call a friend to remind them they're not alone too! Share an encouraging word or a moment of gratitude with them.

My Tender Prayer: "God, teach me to surrender to change and uncertainty with grace, knowing that in my vulnerability, there is room for growth. Help me to open my heart and embrace the unknown, feeling the beauty in surrender. Guide me to trust that in being vulnerable, I allow myself to bloom fully—sensually, emotionally, and spiritually. Amen."

Reflection Prompt: What changes in your life feel overwhelming or intimidating right now? Write about how allowing yourself to be vulnerable in these moments can bring a sense of freedom and help you move through transitions with a deeper connection to your own sensuality and honesty.

October 16: God, Help Me to Seek Comfort in You

Prayer: "Hey God, when life feels overwhelming, help me to seek comfort in friendship and your presence. I know that you're my safe haven, and I want to remember that it's okay to lean on you when things get tough, but also connect deeper with those around me."

Scripture Reference: "The Lord is close to the brokenhearted and saves those who are crushed in spirit." —Psalm 34:18

Contemplation: In what ways can you intentionally seek comfort in God during hard times? How can prayer and scripture bring you solace?

Daily Reminder: "God's presence is my comfort; I will find refuge in Him."

Engaging Prompt: You are worthy beyond all description.

My Tender Prayer: "God, may I learn to communicate my needs openly. Help me express what I require from my relationships. Amen."

Reflection Prompt: What needs do you often suppress? Write about how expressing them could improve your connections with others.

October 17: God, Help Me to Embrace Change

Prayer: "Jesus, change is hard for me. Help me to embrace the changes in my life and trust that you have a plan for each transition. I want to see change as an opportunity for growth."

Scripture Reference: "Jesus Christ is the same yesterday and today and forever." —Hebrews 13:8

Contemplation: What changes are you currently facing? How can you shift your perspective to see them as blessings in disguise?

Daily Reminder: "Change is a part of life, and I will embrace it with an open heart."

Engaging Prompt: Write about a change you're currently experiencing and what potential blessings could come from it. How can you view this change through a lens of faith?

My Tender Prayer: "Lord, teach me to find strength in community. Help me to connect with others who embrace the moment together. Amen."

Reflection Prompt: Who in your community embodies spontaneity? Write about how their openness inspires you.

October 18: God, Help Me to Cultivate a Grateful Heart

Prayer: "Hey God, sometimes I forget to appreciate the good things in my life. Help me to cultivate a heart of gratitude, especially when life feels heavy. I know that gratitude shifts my focus from problems to blessings."

Scripture Reference: "Give thanks in all circumstances; for this is God's will for you in Christ Jesus." —1 Thessalonians 5:18

Contemplation: What are three things you're grateful for today? How does gratitude change your outlook?

Daily Reminder: "Gratitude is my strength; it transforms my perspective."

Engaging Prompt: Tell someone you appreciate them being themselves.

My Tender Prayer: "Dear God, help me to nurture my inner child. May I embrace my softness and allow myself to play and explore. Amen."

Reflection Prompt: What activities make you feel playful and free? Write about how you can incorporate more of these into your life

October 19: God, Help Me to Shine Your Light

Prayer: "Jesus, I want to be a light in this world, especially during dark times. Help me to shine your love and hope to those around me, even when I'm feeling down myself."

Scripture Reference: "You are the light of the world. A town built on a hill cannot be hidden." —Matthew 5:14

Contemplation: How can you be a light for someone else today? What simple acts of kindness can you offer?

Daily Reminder: "I carry God's light within me; I will share it with the world."

Engaging Prompt: Think of one small way you can brighten someone's day today. Write down your plan and make it happen!

My Tender Prayer: "God, help me to honor my past as part of my journey, with all its lessons, freedom, and growth. Teach me that my experiences don't define me, but they've shaped who I am today. Let me embrace every part of my story without shame, knowing that I'm worthy of love and respect in every way. Guide me in using my past as a stepping stone to deeper self-love and a more authentic connection with You. Amen."

Reflection Prompt: Listen to music turned up loud today.

October 20: God, Help Me to Let Go of Grudges

Prayer: "Hey God, holding onto grudges is exhausting. Help me to let go of past hurts and forgive those who've wronged me. I want to free myself from the burden of resentment."

Scripture Reference: "Forgive as the Lord forgave you." —Colossians 3:13

Contemplation: What grudges are you holding onto? How can releasing them improve your mental and emotional health?

Daily Reminder: "Forgiveness is a gift I give myself; I choose peace."

Engaging Prompt: Write a letter (you don't have to send it) to someone you need to forgive. Express your feelings, then focus on letting go.

My Tender Prayer: "Lord, help me accept that vulnerability is a human experience. May I find comfort in sharing this journey with others. Amen."

Reflection Prompt: How can you remind yourself that everyone experiences vulnerability? Write about ways to connect with others in this shared experience.

October 21: God, Help Me to Build Resilience

Prayer: "Jesus, I know that life's trials can either break me or make me stronger. Help me to build resilience and rise up after every fall. I want to learn from my experiences, not be defined by them."

Scripture Reference: "Not only so, but we also glory in our sufferings, because we know that suffering produces perseverance; perseverance, character; and character, hope." —Romans 5:3-4

Contemplation: What experiences have shaped your resilience? How can you use past struggles as steppingstones for future strength?

Daily Reminder: "Every challenge I face is an opportunity for growth; I will rise stronger."

Engaging Prompt: Reflect on a time you overcame a significant challenge. What did you learn about yourself, and how can you apply that lesson now?

My Tender Prayer: "Heavenly Father, thank You for the gift of my emotions, for they are the pulse of my human experience. Help me to embrace them with grace, knowing they shape who I am and how I connect with the world. May I find peace in my feelings, allowing them to flow freely and authentically, and express gratitude for the depth they bring to my soul. Amen."

Reflection Prompt: What emotions do you often take for granted? Reflect on how expressing gratitude for them can enhance your emotional experience.

October 22: God, Help Me to Seek Wisdom

Prayer: "Hey God, I'm looking for wisdom to navigate my current situation. Help me to make choices that reflect your love and truth. I want to be guided by wisdom, not just my feelings."

Scripture Reference: "If any of you lacks wisdom, you should ask God, who gives generously to all without finding fault." —James 1:5

Contemplation: What decision are you struggling with right now? How can seeking God's wisdom change your approach?

Daily Reminder: "God's wisdom lights my path; I will seek it daily."

Engaging Prompt: Take a moment to pray for wisdom regarding a specific decision. Write down your thoughts, and trust that clarity will come.

My Tender Prayer: "God, help me to seek support when I need it. Teach me that reaching out is an act of strength, not weakness. Amen."

Reflection Prompt: When was the last time you reached out for support? Write about how this experience affected you.

October 23: God, Help Me to Embrace My Uniqueness

Prayer: "Jesus, sometimes I struggle to embrace who I am, quirks and all. Help me to see my uniqueness as a gift and to appreciate the person you've created me to be."

Scripture Reference: "I praise you because I am fearfully and wonderfully made." —Psalm 139:14

Contemplation: What makes you unique? How can you celebrate those traits instead of hiding them?

Daily Reminder: "My uniqueness is a gift; I will embrace who I am!"

Engaging Prompt: List five things that make you uniquely you. Celebrate those qualities today—wear your favorite outfit or try something new!

My Tender Prayer: "Lord, may I create boundaries that honor my truth. Teach me to protect my heart while remaining open. Amen."

Reflection Prompt: What boundaries do you need to set in your relationships? Reflect on how these will help you feel safer and more vulnerable.

October 24: God, Help Me to Find Strength in Vulnerability

Prayer: "Hey God, I've always thought of vulnerability as weakness, but I'm realizing it takes strength to be open. Help me to embrace vulnerability as a way to connect with others and show my true self."

Scripture Reference: "My grace is sufficient for you, for my power is made perfect in weakness." —2 Corinthians 12:9

Contemplation: You should get to know your neighbors?

Daily Reminder: "Vulnerability is strength; I will embrace it boldly."

Engaging Prompt: Share a personal story or struggle with someone you trust. How did it feel to be open about your feelings?

My Tender Prayer: "Dear God, may I approach life with curiosity rather than judgment. Help me to explore my feelings without fear. Amen."

Reflection Prompt: Who can I get to know better?

October 25: God, Help Me to Trust in Your Protection

Prayer: "Jesus, my past may be filled with moments I'm not proud of, but I know You see me as I am and love me through it all. Help me find comfort in Your protection, knowing that no matter what challenges or uncertainties come my way, I am never alone. Guide me with Your love, and remind me that I'm worthy of Your grace and care. Amen."

Scripture Reference: "The Lord will fight for you; you need only to be still." —Exodus 14:14

Contemplation: What fears do you need to surrender to God's protection? How can you remind yourself of His constant presence?

Daily Reminder: "God is my protector; I will rest in His assurance."

Engaging Prompt: List three times you felt God's protection in your life. Reflect on how those experiences built your faith.

My Tender Prayer: "God, help me to share my dreams and aspirations with others. May my vulnerability inspire connection and support. Amen."

Reflection Prompt: What dreams feel important to share? Write about how sharing these aspirations can create a supportive community.

October 26: God, Help Me to Celebrate Progress

Prayer: "Hey God, I often focus on where I'm not instead of where I've come from. Help me to celebrate my progress, no matter how small, and recognize the growth you're fostering in me."

Scripture Reference: "Do not despise these small beginnings, for the Lord rejoices to see the work begin." —Zechariah 4:10

Contemplation: What progress have you made lately, big or small? How can celebrating those victories boost your motivation?

Daily Reminder: "Every step forward is worth celebrating; I will acknowledge my progress."

Engaging Prompt: Write down three achievements from the past month. Celebrate them in a fun way—maybe treat yourself to something special!

My Tender Prayer: "Lord, help me to embrace every twist and turn of my journey—every high and every low. Teach me to see the beauty in the chaos, the lessons in the heartache, and the adventure in every challenge. May I always find gratitude for the experiences that have shaped me, making me stronger, more confident, and more unapologetically myself. Let me walk forward with curiosity, knowing that all of it—the good, the bad, the sexy—is part of the beautiful story You're telling through my life. Amen."

Reflection Prompt: What are the wild, unexpected experiences in your life that you're grateful for, even if they were difficult or uncertain at the time? Reflect on how they've shaped you, both in the way you love yourself and the way you navigate life's adventures moving forward.

October 27: God, Help Me to Trust in Your Timing

Prayer: "Jesus, sometimes I'm just ready for things to happen, like *yesterday*. I get impatient, and my timeline feels like the only one that matters. But I know You're working behind the scenes, even when I can't see it. Help me trust in Your perfect timing, and remind me that I don't need to rush. You've got it all figured out—way better than I do! So, I'll hang tight, knowing that what's meant for me is coming at the perfect moment. Amen."

Scripture Reference: "To everything, there is a season and a time for every matter under heaven." —Ecclesiastes 3:1

Contemplation: What areas of your life are you feeling impatient about? How can trusting in God's timing bring you peace?

Daily Reminder: "God's timing is perfect; I will wait with faith."

Engaging Prompt: Write about a time when waiting led to something beautiful in your life. How did that experience shape your understanding of patience?

My Tender Prayer: "Heavenly Father, help me to express my needs with clarity and compassion. May I communicate openly with love. Amen."

Reflection Prompt: How do you currently express your needs? Reflect on how you can communicate them more effectively.

October 28: God, Help Me to Find Joy in the Journey

Prayer: "Hey God, life can sometimes feel more like a struggle than a journey. Help me to find joy in the process, even in the boring in between moments. I want to appreciate the ride instead of just focusing on the destination."

Scripture Reference: "Rejoice in the Lord always. I will say it again: Rejoice!" —Philippians 4:4

Contemplation: What moments in your day can you find joy in? How can you shift your focus from the end goal to the beauty of the journey?

Daily Reminder: "Joy is found in the journey; I will seek it daily."

Engaging Prompt: Take a walk and notice the little things around you that bring you joy—a flower, a smile from a stranger, the sound of laughter. Write them down.

My Tender Prayer: "God, help me honor my past experiences, both the beautiful and the challenging, knowing they've shaped me into the strong, resilient person I am today. Teach me to embrace every part of my journey with grace, understanding, and acceptance. Let me walk forward, fully aware that my past is a part of me, but it doesn't define me—it empowers me. Amen."

Reflection Prompt: What past experiences do you struggle to accept? Write about how honoring them can lead to healing.

October 29: God, Help Me to Nurture My Soul

Prayer: "Jesus, I often neglect my soul while focusing on everything else. Help me to nurture my spirit, taking time for self-care and connection with you. I want to cultivate a deep relationship with you."

Scripture Reference: "But the Lord said to me, 'Do not say, "I am too young." You must go to everyone I send you to and say whatever I command you.'" —Jeremiah 1:7

Contemplation: How can you nurture your soul today? What activities fill your spirit with joy and peace?

Daily Reminder: "Nurturing my soul brings me closer to God; I will prioritize it."

Engaging Prompt: Schedule a self-care day for yourself this week. What will you do to nurture your soul? Write down your plans.

My Tender Prayer: "Lord, help me to be present in the moment and appreciate the beauty of life. May I cultivate a sense of softness and wonder. Amen."

Reflection Prompt: What moments in your day bring you joy? Write about how being present enhances your experience of life.

October 30: God, Help Me to Build Meaningful Connections

Prayer: "Hey God, I want to build deeper connections with those around me. Help me to be open-hearted and present in my relationships, creating spaces where love can flourish."

Scripture Reference: "A friend loves at all times, and a brother is born for a time of adversity." —Proverbs 17:17

Contemplation: What relationships in your life need more attention? How can you invest in those connections?

Daily Reminder: "Meaningful connections enrich my life; I will nurture them."

Engaging Prompt: Reach out to someone you care about and schedule a coffee date or phone call. What do you hope to share or learn from this conversation?

My Tender Prayer: "Dear God, thank You for the lessons learned through connections with others. May I continue to grow in love and acceptance. Amen."

Reflection Prompt: Cook something warm and comforting.

October 31: God, Help Me to End This Month with Purpose

Prayer: "Hey Jesus, as this month wraps up, help me take a moment to look back and have a little fun with how much I've grown. It's been a wild ride, and I'm here for all the lessons, the wins, and even the mess-ups. Help me carry all this good energy into next month, ready to make it even better. I'm all about learning, growing, and keeping it light. Let's do this! Amen."

Scripture Reference: "Forget the former things; do not dwell on the past. See, I am doing a new thing!" —Isaiah 43:18-19

Contemplation: What lessons have you learned this month? How can you carry those insights into your next steps?

Daily Reminder: "Love Yourself."

Engaging Prompt: Write a letter to your future self, outlining your hopes and goals for the upcoming month. Seal it and read it at the end of the next month!

My Tender Prayer: "Hey God, as this month wraps up, help me carry the sensuality, strength, and confidence I've tapped into with me into next month. I've embraced my softness and my power, and I'm ready to keep leveling up. Show me how to stay bold, unapologetically feminine, and open to the adventure of it all. Let me move forward with grace, fire, and the freedom to just *be* me—every part of me. Amen."

Reflection Prompt: What parts of your femininity and sensuality have you embraced this month? Write about how you can continue to nurture those sides of yourself, staying playful, confident, and fully present in your own body and soul.

November: Gratitude & Grace

November invites us to embrace the power of gratitude and how it can transform the way we see the world. When we focus on what we have rather than what we lack, our hearts open to the abundance of blessings God has already placed in our lives. This month encourages us to develop a habit of thankfulness, appreciating the people, experiences, and lessons that have shaped us. Through gratitude, we create space for God's grace to move in our hearts, reminding us that each moment is part of His greater plan for our journey forward.

As we step into November, a month often dedicated to gratitude and Contemplation, let's take a moment to appreciate where we've come from and how far we've traveled. In a world that often demands more from us, it's essential to pause, breathe, and acknowledge the blessings in our lives, even amidst the chaos. This month, we'll focus on recognizing the good, nurturing gratitude, and creating a space for reflection. We'll also remember that every experience, no matter how spicy or challenging, has shaped us into the resilient women we are today. Let's dive into the month with open hearts, ready to celebrate both the big wins and the small joys that remind us we are loved and worthy.

November 1: God, Thank You for New Beginnings

Prayer: "Hey God, as we step into this new month, I want to thank you for new beginnings. Help me to embrace the opportunities that lie ahead and to appreciate the fresh start that November brings."

Scripture Reference: "Therefore, if anyone is in Christ, the new creation has come: The old has gone, the new is here!" —2 Corinthians 5:17

Contemplation: What does newness feel like?

Daily Reminder: "Every day is a chance to start anew; I will embrace it!"

Engaging Prompt: Write about a new beginning you're experiencing or hope to experience this month. How can you welcome this change into your life?

My Tender Prayer: "Dear God, thank You for the gift of my body, mind, and spirit. Help me appreciate the person I am today. Amen."

Reflection Prompt: What unique qualities make you who you are? Write or draw something that represents your individuality.

November 2: God, Help Me to Appreciate the Little Things

Prayer: "Jesus, in the hustle and bustle of life, it's easy to overlook the little things. Help me to pause and appreciate the small joys that brighten my days, from a warm cup of coffee to a genuine smile."

Scripture Reference: "Every good and perfect gift is from above." —James 1:17

Contemplation: What little things bring you joy? How can you make someone else smile?

Daily Reminder: "Life's little joys are treasures; I will cherish them."

Engaging Prompt: Make a list of ten small things you're grateful for today. How do these items uplift your spirit?

My Tender Prayer: "Lord, may I cultivate a grateful heart. Teach me to see the beauty within myself and in the world around me. Amen."

Reflection Prompt: take a moment and really look at yourself in the mirror, without judgement.

November 3: God, Help Me to Find Joy in the Everyday Things

Prayer: "Hey God, sometimes daily tasks feel mundane, and I forget to find joy in them. Help me to see the beauty in the everyday moments and to approach each task with happiness as well as gratitude."

Scripture Reference: "Whatever you do, work at it with all your heart, as working for the Lord." —Colossians 3:23

Contemplation: What mundane tasks can you view through a lens of gratitude? How can this shift enhance your daily life?

Daily Reminder: "Even the mundane has beauty; I will find joy in it."

Engaging Prompt: Choose a mundane task (like doing laundry or cooking) and approach it with mindfulness and faith. What can you learn from this experience?

My Tender Prayer: "Heavenly Father, help me honor my body by treating it with love and respect. May I find new ways to nurture it as a sacred vessel. Amen."

Reflection Prompt: What are three ways you can care for your body today? Decide to incorporate them into your day.

November 4: God, Help Me to Express My Gratitude

Prayer: "Jesus, gratitude is meant to be shared. Help me to express my thankfulness to others, reminding them how much they mean to me and how their presence enriches my life."

Scripture Reference: "Let the peace of Christ rule in your hearts, since as members of one body you were called to peace. And be thankful." —Colossians 3:15

Contemplation: Who in your life deserves your gratitude? How can you communicate this to them effectively?

Daily Reminder: "Expressing gratitude strengthens connections; I will share it."

Engaging Prompt: Write a thank-you note or message to someone who has impacted your life positively. How do you feel after expressing your gratitude?

My Tender Prayer: "Hey God, show me the power in my vulnerabilities. Help me see how they've made me stronger, fiercer, and more unapologetically me. Let me embrace every moment where I've opened up, knowing it's just another layer of who I am. Teach me to love every part of me, even the messy, vulnerable bits. Amen."

Reflection Prompt: Think about a vulnerability you've faced head-on. How did it transform you and build your strength? Write about how that experience has made you more confident, bolder, and more comfortable in your own skin.

November 5: God, Help Me to Let Go of Negativity

Prayer: "Hey God, negativity can be so overwhelming at times. Help me to let go of the habit of negative thoughts that weigh me down and to instead focus on the positive aspects of my life instead."

Scripture Reference: "Finally, brothers and sisters, whatever is true, whatever is noble, whatever is right, whatever is pure, whatever is lovely, whatever is admirable—if anything is excellent or praiseworthy—think about such things." —Philippians 4:8

Contemplation: What negative thoughts do you need to release? How can shifting your focus to positivity transform your mindset?

Daily Reminder: "I choose to focus on the positive; negativity will not control me."

Engaging Prompt: How do your thoughts affect your mood?

My Tender Prayer: "Hey Lord, thanks for the lessons hidden in all the tough stuff. Help me see those challenges not as setbacks but as juicy opportunities to level up. I'm ready to take on whatever comes my way, knowing that every curveball is just another chance to grow and glow. Amen."

Reflection Prompt: What tough experience ended up teaching you something you never expected? Write about how it's shaped the fierce, confident, and fabulous person you are today.

November 6: God, Help Me to See Challenges as Opportunities

Prayer: "Jesus, life throws obstacles my way, and sometimes I see them as roadblocks. Help me to view each challenge as an opportunity for growth and learning instead."

Scripture Reference: "Consider it pure joy, my brothers and sisters, whenever you face trials of many kinds." —James 1:2

Contemplation: Can daily challenges be seen as a sport?

Daily Reminder: "Challenges lead to growth; I will embrace them."

Engaging Prompt: Ask someone else what their goals are.

My Tender Prayer: "Dear God, may I practice self-compassion. Teach me to speak kindly to myself and appreciate my efforts. Amen."

Reflection Prompt: I have challenging goals that help me grow.

November 7: God, Help Me to Practice Self-Compassion

Prayer: "Hey God, I often struggle with being hard on myself. Help me to practice self-compassion and to treat myself with the same kindness I would offer to a friend."

Scripture Reference: "Be kind to one another, tenderhearted, forgiving one another, as God in Christ forgave you." —Ephesians 4:32

Contemplation: Can you add some feel-good music to your inner soundtrack?

Daily Reminder: "Self-compassion is a gift I will give myself today."

Engaging Prompt: Draw something happy, rather something that makes you feel happy while drawing it.

My Tender Prayer: "God, help me see my body as a source of strength and beauty. May I honor it for all it does for me. Amen."

Reflection Prompt: List three things your body allows you to do. Reflect on how you can show gratitude for these abilities.

November 8: God, Help Me to Cultivate a Heart of Gratitude

Prayer: "Jesus, I want my heart to overflow with gratitude. Help me to cultivate a grateful spirit that sees the goodness around me, even when life feels heavy."

Scripture Reference: "Give thanks to the Lord, for he is good; his love endures forever." —Psalm 107:1

Contemplation: When you first wake up what is your perspective? Can you improve it?

Daily Reminder: "A grateful heart is a magnet for miracles."

Engaging Prompt: Start a gratitude jar—write down things you're thankful for throughout the month and read them at the end of the year.

My Tender Prayer: "Lord, thank You for the loving support of my community, for the hearts that surround me with kindness and care. Help me to truly see and feel the love that lifts me up, reminding me that I am never alone. Let me be open to receiving the warmth of those around me, and may I give that same love in return. Amen."

Reflection Prompt: Who in your life are you grateful for? Write a note of appreciation to them, expressing your gratitude.

November 9: God, Help Me to Reflect on My Blessings

Prayer: "Hey God, I want to take time to reflect on my blessings, both big and small. Help me to see how richly I've been blessed, whether in quiet moments or during wild times and late nights."

Scripture Reference: "Every good and perfect gift is from above." —James 1:17

Contemplation: Sometimes we do not recognize blessings until later.

Daily Reminder: "I will count my blessings and let gratitude fill my heart."

Engaging Prompt: List five blessings you're thankful for today. How do these blessings impact your outlook on life?

My Tender Prayer: "Heavenly Father, thank You for this wild, unpredictable journey I'm on. Help me embrace every twist and turn, every unexpected moment, and celebrate how each step has led me here. Teach me to trust that even the messy, uncertain parts of my path are exactly where I'm meant to be. Let me walk boldly forward, knowing that my journey is uniquely mine, and it's shaping me into who I'm meant to be. Amen."

Reflection Prompt: The past mistakes I made weren't always that bad.

November 10: God, Help Me to Appreciate My Journey

Prayer: "Jesus, my journey has been anything but ordinary. Help me to appreciate the path I've traveled, with all its twists and turns, as part of your divine plan for my life."

Scripture Reference: "For I know the thoughts that I think toward you, says the Lord, thoughts of peace and not of evil, to give you a future and a hope." —Jeremiah 29:11

Contemplation: Time is always filled.

Daily Reminder: "Distractions can lead to new experiences."

Engaging Prompt: Call a friend.

My Tender Prayer: "God, help me appreciate the beauty in the stories of those around me as I learn about their experiences or opinions. Teach me to honor the differences that make us all unique. Amen."

Reflection Prompt: why is celebration so important?

November 11: God, Help Me to Serve Others with Gratitude

Prayer: "Hey God, I want to express my gratitude through action. Help me to serve others with a grateful heart, sharing your love and blessings with those around me."

Scripture Reference: "Serve one another humbly in love." —Galatians 5:13

Contemplation: Make something nice for someone else.

Daily Reminder: "Serving others is an expression of my gratitude; I will do it joyfully."

Engaging Prompt: Identify one way you can serve someone in your life this week. Plan your action and see how it impacts both of you.

My Tender Prayer: "Lord, thank You for my creativity. May I embrace it as a gift and use it to express my authentic self. Amen."

Reflection Prompt: What creative outlets bring you joy? Plan time today to engage in one of them.

November 12: God, Help Me to Find Peace in the Present

Prayer: "Jesus, it's easy to get caught up in worries about the future. Help me to find peace in the present moment, appreciating the here and now."

Scripture Reference: "Do not worry about tomorrow, for tomorrow will worry about itself. Each day has enough trouble of its own." —Matthew 6:34

Contemplation: What thoughts or worries are keeping you from being present? How can you let go of them?

Daily Reminder: "I choose peace in the present; I will not be anxious."

Engaging Prompt: Practice mindfulness for five minutes today. What do you notice about your thoughts and feelings in this moment?

My Tender Prayer: "Dear God, help me celebrate my achievements, both big and small. May I recognize the hard work behind each one. Amen."

Reflection Prompt: List three achievements you are proud of. Reflect on the effort and dedication that went into achieving them.

November 13: God, Help Me to Let Go of Comparisons

Prayer: "Hey God, sometimes I catch myself looking at others and thinking I should be more like them. But You made me *me*, and that's enough. Help me to rock my own journey with confidence, embrace all my quirks, and celebrate my individuality. I'm ready to stop comparing and start owning my fabulousness. Amen."

Scripture Reference: "For we are God's handiwork, created in Christ Jesus to do good works, which God prepared in advance for us to do." —Ephesians 2:10

Contemplation: What comparisons do you struggle with? How can embracing your uniqueness free you from this cycle?

Daily Reminder: "I am uniquely made; I will celebrate my individuality."

Engaging Prompt: Write down three things that make you unique. How can you embrace these qualities in your daily life?

My Tender Prayer: "God, help me uncover the beauty and joy woven into this very moment. Teach me to savor life as it gently unfolds, one breath, one heartbeat, one day at a time. May I embrace the softness of now, finding peace in its rhythm and delight in its simplicity. Amen."

Reflection Prompt: What small joys did you experience today? Write about how they made you feel.

November 14: God, Help Me to Celebrate Others' Successes

Prayer: "Jesus, jealousy can creep in when I see others succeed. Help me to celebrate their achievements and recognize that we are all on our own paths."

Scripture Reference: "Rejoice with those who rejoice; mourn with those who mourn." —Romans 12:15

Contemplation: How can celebrating others' successes change your perspective? What steps can you take to foster this attitude?

Daily Reminder: "Celebrating others enriches my life; I will rejoice with them."

Engaging Prompt: Reach out to someone in your life who has achieved something significant. Share your excitement and celebrate with them!

My Tender Prayer: "Lord, help me release comparisons and embrace my uniqueness. May I focus on my journey, not others'. Amen."

Reflection Prompt: When do you find yourself comparing to others? Write about how you can shift your focus to your own path.

November 15: God, Help Me to Make Time for Gratitude

Prayer: "Hey God, I'm ready to turn gratitude into my daily mood. Help me make it a habit to look around and see all the blessings—big, small, and everything in between. From my wildest dreams to the little moments that make me smile, I want to soak it all in and say thank you. Let me be the kind of woman who radiates appreciation for every good thing in my life. Amen."

Scripture Reference: "Give thanks in all circumstances; for this is God's will for you in Christ Jesus." —1 Thessalonians 5:18

Contemplation: Noticing the good life increases it.

Daily Reminder: "Gratitude is a practice; I will cultivate it daily."

Engaging Prompt: Say it out loud.

My Tender Prayer: "Heavenly Father, thank You for the resilience that has carried me through even my hardest moments. My past may not be perfect, but it's mine, and I'm learning to embrace every piece of it. Help me to see my strength clearly and appreciate how far I've come. Teach me to honor the growth born from my challenges and to walk forward with gratitude and grace. Amen."

Reflection Prompt: Reflect on a challenging time when you showed resilience. What did you learn about yourself through this experience?

November 16: God, Help Me to Focus on What Matters

Prayer: "Jesus, life can be distracting, pulling me in different directions. Help me to focus on what truly matters and to invest my time and energy wisely."

Scripture Reference: "Set your minds on things that are above, not on things that are on earth." —Colossians 3:2

Contemplation: What matters most to you? How can you align your daily actions with these values?

Daily Reminder: "I will focus on what matters; distractions will not derail me."

Engaging Prompt: Identify your top three priorities this month. How will you ensure you dedicate time and energy to them?

My Tender Prayer: "God, thank You for the gift of self-discovery. May I continue to explore who I am and who I'm becoming. Amen."

Reflection Prompt: What have you learned about yourself recently? Write about how this insight impacts your life.

November 17: God, Help Me to Cultivate a Grateful Attitude

Prayer: "Hey God, cultivating gratitude is a daily choice. Help me to adopt a grateful attitude that reflects your love and goodness in my life."

Scripture Reference: "Let them give thanks to the Lord for his unfailing love and his wonderful deeds for mankind." —Psalm 107:8

Contemplation: How can you shift your mindset to focus on gratitude? What practices will support this attitude?

Daily Reminder: "A grateful attitude attracts blessings; I will cultivate it."

Engaging Prompt: Try starting or ending each day by listing things you're grateful for. How does this shift your perspective?

My Tender Prayer: "Lord, may I appreciate my body for its uniqueness. Teach me to see my beauty through Your eyes. Amen."

Reflection Prompt: What do you love most about your physical appearance? Write about how these features make you feel.

November 18: God, Help Me to Reflect on My Growth

Prayer: "Hey Jesus, I'm here to take a moment and look back at all the ways I've grown this year. Help me see how each twist and turn, the highs and the lows, have shaped me into this confident, evolving woman I'm becoming. Let me embrace every lesson, every moment, and know that all of it has made me stronger, sexier, and more beautifully myself. I'm ready to carry that power into the next chapter. Amen."

Scripture Reference: "But grow in the grace and knowledge of our Lord and Savior Jesus Christ." —2 Peter 3:18

Contemplation: What will I think when I look back on this moment?

Daily Reminder: "Contemplation fuels growth; I will honor my journey."

Engaging Prompt: Write a letter to your past self, acknowledging your growth and what you've learned. How does it feel to reflect on this?

My Tender Prayer: "Dear God, help me recognize the importance of self-care. May I prioritize my well-being with love and intention. Amen."

Reflection Prompt: How does dressing well change how I show up in the world.

November 19: God, Help Me to Stay Grounded in Gratitude

Prayer: "Hey God, it's easy to get caught up in the chaos of life. Help me to stay grounded in gratitude, allowing it to anchor me amidst the storms."

Scripture Reference: "Let your roots grow down into him, and let your lives be built on him." —Colossians 2:7

Contemplation: What practices help you stay grounded? How can gratitude serve as your anchor?

Daily Reminder: "Gratitude anchors my soul; I will remain grounded."

Engaging Prompt: Relationships can be grounding too.

My Tender Prayer: "God, may I express gratitude for the lessons learned from failure. Help me see them as steppingstones to success. Amen."

Reflection Prompt: What failures have taught you valuable lessons? Reflect on how these experiences have shaped your journey.

November 20: God, Help Me to Release Grudges

Prayer: "Jesus, holding onto grudges weighs me down. Help me to release any anger or bitterness and to embrace forgiveness for my peace."

Scripture Reference: "For if you forgive other people when they sin against you, your heavenly Father will also forgive you." —Matthew 6:14

Contemplation: What grudges are you holding onto? How can releasing them free your spirit?

Daily Reminder: "Forgiveness sets me free; I will let go."

Engaging Prompt: Identify one person you need to forgive. Write them a letter (you don't have to send it) to express your feelings and release the burden.

My Tender Prayer: "Hey Lord, I like being me, and through all my past experiences and relationships, I want to embrace who I am today, flaws and all. Let me see myself as You see me—strong, beautiful, and worthy. Amen."

Reflection Prompt: Call a relative today.

November 21: God, Help Me to Find Strength in Vulnerability

Prayer: "Hey God, being vulnerable is scary, but it's also where I find connection and strength. Help me to embrace vulnerability as a source of empowerment."

Scripture Reference: "My grace is sufficient for you, for my power is made perfect in weakness." —2 Corinthians 12:9

Contemplation: Some surfaces are thermal conductors.

Daily Reminder: "Vulnerability is strength; I will embrace it."

Engaging Prompt: Share something vulnerable with a trusted friend today. How does this experience strengthen your bond?

My Tender Prayer: "Heavenly Father, help me appreciate my strength, both physical and emotional. May I honor my capabilities with gratitude. Amen."

Reflection Prompt: List three things you consider your strengths. How do they empower you in your daily life?

November 22: God, Help Me to Cultivate a Grateful Heart

Prayer: "Jesus, help me to cultivate a grateful heart that sees your blessings in every situation. I want my heart to overflow with gratitude, no matter what life throws my way."

Scripture Reference: "Be thankful in all circumstances." —1 Thessalonians 5:18

Contemplation: How can cultivating a grateful heart change your perspective on challenges? What practices can you adopt to nurture this heart?

Daily Reminder: "A grateful heart radiates positivity; I will nurture it."

Engaging Prompt: Make a date night for yourself, getting ready like you would for a lover, really treat yourself special.

My Tender Prayer: "God, help me honor the fierce journey of self-love I've been on. Guide me to recognize the growth I've made, no matter how small, and embrace the beauty in every step I've taken. I'm ready to fully own who I am—inside and out—and keep loving myself with courage, confidence, and grace. Amen."

Reflection Prompt: What bold moves have you made toward loving yourself more? Reflect on how each step has shifted the way you see yourself and the world around you.

November 23: God, Help Me to Live with Intentionality

Prayer: "Hey God, I want to live intentionally, making choices that reflect my values and desires. Help me to be mindful of my actions and their impact."

Scripture Reference: "Whatever you do, do it all for the glory of God." —1 Corinthians 10:31

Contemplation: How can you bring more intention into your daily life? What choices reflect your core values?

Daily Reminder: "Living intentionally enriches my life; I will choose wisely."

Engaging Prompt: What do you really want?

My Tender Prayer: "Lord, thank You for my passions. Help me to pursue them with joy and enthusiasm. Amen."

Reflection Prompt: What are your passions? Write about how you can incorporate them more into your life.

November 24: God, Help Me to Seek Your Guidance

Prayer: "Jesus, I want to seek your guidance in every aspect of my life. Help me to trust your wisdom and lean on you for direction."

Scripture Reference: "Trust in the Lord with all your heart, and He will make your paths straight." —Proverbs 3:5

Contemplation: What decisions do you need guidance on? How can seeking God's wisdom lead you to peace?

Daily Reminder: "God's guidance illuminates my path; I will seek it."

Engaging Prompt: Spend time in prayer, asking for God's guidance on a specific decision. Write down what you feel led to do.

My Tender Prayer: "Dear God, help me to appreciate my imperfections. Teach me to see them as beautiful parts of my humanity. Amen."

Reflection Prompt: What imperfections do you struggle to accept? Write about how embracing them can lead to self-acceptance. -

November 25: God, Help Me to Celebrate My Progress

Prayer: "Hey God, I want to celebrate my progress, both big and small. Help me to recognize and appreciate the steps I've taken on my journey."

Scripture Reference: "Do not despise these small beginnings, for the Lord rejoices to see the work begin." —Zechariah 4:10

Contemplation: Think back to before you knew which steps to take, and how much easier things became once you had some guidance.

Daily Reminder: "Celebrating progress fuels my motivation; I will honor it."

Engaging Prompt: Write down three achievements, no matter how small. How can you celebrate them?

My Tender Prayer: "Hey God, thanks for this rollercoaster ride I call my life. Whether it's been a total win or a situation, I know there's a lesson hiding somewhere. So, guide me to find the humor in the chaos and gratitude for the lessons. Amen."

Reflection Prompt: Sing in the car.

November 26: God, Help Me to Nurture My Relationships

Prayer: "Jesus, relationships are a source of joy and connection. Help me to nurture the relationships in my life and to express gratitude to those I love."

Scripture Reference: "Above all, love each other deeply, because love covers over a multitude of sins." —1 Peter 4:8

Contemplation: How can you nurture your relationships this month? What actions will show your gratitude?

Daily Reminder: "Nurturing relationships enriches my life; I will invest in them."

Engaging Prompt: Plan a special gesture for someone you care about this week. How will you express your gratitude for their presence in your life?

My Tender Prayer: "Lord, thank You for the amazing, messy, wild love and support I've got in my life. Help me not just to notice it but to actually *show up* and appreciate the ones who keep cheering me on—even when I'm all over the place. Teach me to be as uplifting to them as they are to me, and to make room for all the good vibes You're sending my way. Amen."

Reflection Prompt: Write about someone who has been a source of support for you. How can you express your gratitude to them?

November 27: God, Help Me to Find Joy in Service

Prayer: "Hey God, serving others is a beautiful way to express gratitude. Help me to find joy in serving those around me and to spread kindness."

Scripture Reference: "Each of you should use whatever gift you have received to serve others, as faithful stewards of God's grace." —1 Peter 4:10

Contemplation: What brings you joy in serving others? How can you incorporate this joy into your daily life?

Daily Reminder: "Joy in service spreads love; I will embrace it."

Engaging Prompt: Identify a local charity or organization you can volunteer for this month. How does the idea of serving others make you feel?

My Tender Prayer: "Hey God, help me to embrace the full essence of my femininity and sensuality. Teach me to feel confident in my body and at peace with who I am, unapologetically. May I always find comfort in honoring my sensuality and authenticity, knowing that You made me beautifully and powerfully. Amen."

Reflection Prompt: What practices or moments make you feel connected to your feminine energy and sensual self? Plan to create space for one of these today.

November 28: God, Help Me to Practice Presence

Prayer: "Jesus, help me embrace the gift of being present in every moment. In a world full of distractions, teach me to focus on the here and now, especially in my relationships. May I appreciate the beauty of each interaction and savor each precious second, knowing that today holds all the grace I need. Amen."

Scripture Reference: "Therefore do not be anxious about tomorrow, for tomorrow will be anxious for itself. Let the day's own trouble be sufficient for the day." —Matthew 6:34

Contemplation: What distracts you from being present? How can you eliminate those distractions to fully embrace the moment?

Daily Reminder: "It happens today."

Engaging Prompt: Try a 'digital detox' for a few hours today. How does being present feel?

My Tender Prayer: "Hey God, thanks for making me the quirky, fabulous masterpiece that I am. Remind me that my unique sparkle isn't just okay—it's kind of the point. Teach me to own my gifts, rock my weirdness, and shine like the total star You created me to be. Amen."

Reflection Prompt: What's your secret sauce—the thing that makes you undeniably *you*? Write about how you can strut that uniqueness confidently and let it inspire the people around you.

November 29: God, Help Me to Embrace Change

Prayer: "Hey God, change can be wild—like jumping into the deep end with no floaties. But I know it's where the magic happens. Help me face it head-on with a brave heart, a thankful soul, and maybe even a laugh or two. Remind me that growth is worth the awkward moments and the detours. Amen."

Scripture Reference: "Be strong and courageous. Do not be afraid; do not be discouraged, for the Lord your God will be with you wherever you go." —Joshua 1:9

Contemplation: What changes are you currently facing? How can gratitude help you navigate these transitions?

Daily Reminder: "Change leads to growth; I will embrace it."

Engaging Prompt: Write about a recent change you've experienced. How did it lead to personal growth or a new perspective?

My Tender Prayer: "Hey God, so... what exactly where You going for with some of those life plot twists? Because wow. But seriously, thanks for every bump, curve, and questionable detour—they've shaped me into someone I'm starting to really like. Help me to see the beauty in becoming. Amen."

Reflection Prompt: Which "What just happened?" moments in life have made you who you are today? Reflect on how those twists have helped you grow and evolve.

November 30: God, Help Me to End the Month with Gratitude

Prayer: "Jesus, as November wraps up its cozy vibes and December sparkles into view, fill my heart with gratitude for all the lessons, laughter, and even the messy moments. Help me carry this thankful spirit into the holiday magic and the fresh start ahead. Amen."

Scripture Reference: "Give thanks to the Lord, for he is good; his love endures forever." —Psalm 107:1

Contemplation: How can you carry the spirit of everyday being just like Christmas?

Daily Reminder: "You are loved."

Engaging Prompt: Reflect on the most impactful moments from this month. How can you take these lessons into December?

My Tender Prayer: "God, thank You for teaching me to see myself through eyes of love and kindness. Help me to keep nurturing this journey of gratitude, grace, and a little extra sass. Amen."

Reflection Prompt: How do you think about others when you see them?
With gratitude as our guiding theme for November, let's embrace every moment, celebrating the blessings and lessons that life has to offer. Remember, each day is an opportunity to reflect on our experiences, nurture our relationships, and cultivate a spirit of thankfulness that enriches our lives. Let us carry our gratitude into every action and interaction, allowing it to radiate from our hearts and into the world around us.

December: Redemption & Growth

December invites us to reflect on the themes of redemption and renewal, closing the year with purpose and hope. It's a time to look back on how far we've come, celebrating the lessons learned along the way. This sacred season reminds us that our past doesn't define us but can be a steppingstone toward growth and transformation. As we prepare for a new chapter, we'll explore how to carry the wisdom into the year ahead, embracing the truth that every ending holds the promise of a new beginning.

December: Redemption & Growth

As we step into December, we find ourselves at the end of another year—a time to reflect, celebrate, and embrace the theme of redemption and growth. This month is about recognizing the beauty in our journeys, the lessons learned, and the grace that envelops us in every season. Here, we will honor our past, understanding that it shapes us, but it does not define us. Each entry this month will guide us to reclaim our stories, celebrate our progress, and acknowledge the growth that comes from challenges and triumphs alike.

December 1: God, Help Me to Acknowledge My Journey

Prayer: "Hey God, as December begins, I want to acknowledge my journey this year. Help me to see the lessons and blessings in every experience I've faced."

Scripture Reference: "Remember the wonders he has done, his miracles, and the judgments he pronounced." —1 Chronicles 16:12

Contemplation: What significant moments stand out from this year? How have they shaped who you are today?

Daily Reminder: "My journey is unique; I will honor every step."

Engaging Prompt: Create a timeline of your year, marking key events and lessons learned. What do you notice about your growth?

My Tender Prayer: "Dear God, thank You for the gift of a new month. May I embrace this time of rebirth and renewal with an open heart. Amen."

Reflection Prompt: What does rebirth mean to you? Write or draw your vision of personal renewal this month.

December 2: God, Help Me to Embrace Change with Grace

Prayer: "Jesus, let's be real—change can be terrifying and a little chaotic. But I trust that You're weaving something beautiful in my life. Help me to face these shifts with grace, courage, and maybe even a little excitement, knowing Your plans are always good. Amen."

Scripture Reference: "And we know that in all things God works for the good of those who love him, who have been called according to his purpose." —Romans 8:28

Contemplation: How can you love yourself a little more?

Daily Reminder: "Change leads to growth; I will embrace it with grace."

Engaging Prompt: Identify one change you're facing. How can you frame this change as an opportunity for growth?

My Tender Prayer: "Lord, help me release what no longer serves me. Teach me to make space for new beginnings and opportunities. Amen."

Reflection Prompt: What is one thing you're ready to let go of? Write about how releasing it can create space for growth.

December 3: God, Help Me to Let Go of Regret

Prayer: "Hey God, holding onto regret is heavy. Help me to release what no longer serves me, knowing that I am redeemed through your grace."

Scripture Reference: "Therefore, if anyone is in Christ, the new creation has come: The old has gone, the new is here!" —2 Corinthians 5:17

Contemplation: What regrets are you holding onto? How can letting go of them free you to embrace new possibilities?

Daily Reminder: "I am a new creation; I will let go of regret."

Engaging Prompt: Write a letter to your past self, offering forgiveness and understanding. What would you say?

My Tender Prayer: "Lord, You've crafted me with love and purpose. Help me embrace the beauty and strength You've placed within me. May I shine with a grace that reflects Your light, sharing love, softness, and kindness in all I do. Amen."

Reflection Prompt: What makes someone authentic?

December 4: God, Help Me to Cultivate Hope

Prayer: "Jesus, hope is a powerful force. Help me to cultivate hope in my heart, trusting in your promises for my future."

Scripture Reference: "May the God of hope fill you with all joy and peace as you trust in him." —Romans 15:13

Contemplation: What dreams and aspirations do you have for the future? How can hope fuel your journey?

Daily Reminder: "Hope lights my path; I will nurture it."

Engaging Prompt: Talk to someone about what they hope to accomplish in the new year.

My Tender Prayer: "Sweet God, thank You for the gentle lessons this year has gifted me. Help me carry them with grace into the new year, with a heart full of gratitude and an openness to the beauty You have yet to reveal. Amen."

Reflection Prompt: What tender lesson have you learned this year that has touched your heart? Reflect on how you can carry that wisdom forward with love and grace in the year ahead.

December 5: God, Help Me to Accept My Flaws

Prayer: "Hey God, I know I'm not perfect, and that's okay. Help me to accept my flaws as part of my journey and to see the beauty in imperfection."

Scripture Reference: "Cast all your anxiety on him because he cares for you." —1 Peter 5:7

Contemplation: Do flowers know they are beautiful?

Daily Reminder: "I am beautifully imperfect; I will embrace my flaws."

Engaging Prompt: List three of your imperfections. How can they serve as opportunities for growth or learning?

My Tender Prayer: "God, help me to embrace the powerful beauty of my transformation. May I see each change as a step toward a more sensual, confident, and radiant version of myself. Amen."

Reflection Prompt: How have your personal changes deepened your connection with your femininity? Write about how embracing your sensuality has shaped your journey toward self-love and confidence.

December 6: God, Help Me to Celebrate My Achievements

Prayer: "Hey Jesus, I'm ready to give myself some credit! Help me celebrate all my wins, big and small. Teach me to honor my growth and appreciate the hustle I put in. Amen."

Scripture Reference: "Let us not become weary in doing good, for at the proper time we will reap a harvest if we do not give up." —Galatians 6:9

Contemplation: What achievements are you proud of this year? How can you celebrate these victories?

Daily Reminder: "Every achievement is worth celebrating; I will honor my progress."

Engaging Prompt: Plan a small celebration for yourself this week. What will you do to honor your achievements?

My Tender Prayer: "Dear God, thank You for the strength to rise again after challenges. Help me to trust in my ability to overcome. Amen."

Reflection Prompt: Reflect on a challenge you faced this year. How did it help you grow stronger?

December 7: God, Help Me to Seek Redemption

Prayer: "Hey God, redemption is a powerful gift. Help me to seek it in my life and to extend grace to others as you have extended it to me."

Scripture Reference: "If we confess our sins, he is faithful and just and will forgive us our sins and purify us from all unrighteousness." —1 John 1:9

Contemplation: What areas of your life need redemption? How can you seek healing and restoration?

Daily Reminder: "Redemption is possible; I will embrace it."

Engaging Prompt: Identify one aspect of your life where you seek redemption. What steps can you take to pursue healing?

My Tender Prayer: "God, may I nurture the seeds of hope within me. Help me to trust that new beginnings are possible. Amen."

Reflection Prompt: What hopes do you have for the future? Write about how you can nurture these hopes in the coming weeks.

December 8: God, Help Me to Build Healthy Relationships

Prayer: "Jesus, healthy relationships are essential for growth. Help me to cultivate connections that reflect your love and grace."

Scripture Reference: "Let us consider how we may spur one another on toward love and good deeds." —Hebrews 10:24

Contemplation: What qualities do you seek in your relationships? How can you foster these qualities in your connections?

Daily Reminder: "Healthy relationships nourish my soul; I will cultivate them."

Engaging Prompt: Reach out to a friend or loved one today. How can you express appreciation for their presence in your life?

My Tender Prayer: "Lord, thank You for the support of my loved ones. Help me to show appreciation for their love and encouragement. Amen."

Reflection Prompt: Who has been a source of support for you this year? Write a note of gratitude to them.

December 9: God, Help Me to Learn from My Mistakes

Prayer: "Hey God, mistakes are part of life, but they don't define me. Help me to learn from my mistakes and grow through them."

Scripture Reference: "For the Lord disciplines the one he loves and chastises every son whom he receives." —Hebrews 12:6

Contemplation: What mistakes have you made this year? How can you reframe them as lessons learned?

Daily Reminder: "Mistakes are lessons in disguise; I will learn from them."

Engaging Prompt: Reflect on a mistake you've made this year. What did you learn, and how will it shape your future choices?

My Tender Prayer: "Dear God, may I dance in the quiet beauty of life, finding joy in the smallest of moments. Help me to savor the elegance in everyday pleasures. Amen."

Reflection Prompt: What little moments made your heart smile today? Write about how you can invite more of those sweet, simple joys into your life.

December 10: God, Help Me to Let Go of Control

Prayer: "Jesus, I often want to control every aspect of my life. Help me to release my need for control and to trust in your divine plan."

Scripture Reference: "Trust in the Lord with all your heart and lean not on your own understanding." —Proverbs 3:5

Contemplation: What areas of your life do you struggle to surrender? How can trust in God's plan bring you peace?

Daily Reminder: "Releasing control frees my spirit; I will trust in God."

Engaging Prompt: Identify one area where you need to let go of control. How can you practice surrendering this to God?

My Tender Prayer: "God, may I find beauty in my journey, both the highs and lows. Help me to appreciate each step along the way. Amen."

Reflection Prompt: What has been a beautiful moment in your journey this year? Write about how it shaped your perspective.

December 11: God, Help Me to Embrace New Beginnings

Prayer: "Hey God, every ending is a new beginning. Help me to embrace new opportunities and to view them as chances for growth."

Scripture Reference: "Forget the former things; do not dwell on the past. See, I am doing a new thing!" —Isaiah 43:18-19

Contemplation: What new beginnings are you facing this month? How can you approach them with excitement and hope?

Daily Reminder: "New beginnings bring growth; I will embrace them."

Engaging Prompt: Write down three new beginnings you're excited about. How can you approach them with enthusiasm?

My Tender Prayer: "Lord, help me embrace my inner light, my soft graces, my tender parts. Teach me to share my gifts with the world and inspire others. Amen."

Reflection Prompt. You can cultivate any area of interest you have inside of you.

December 12: God, Help Me to Practice Self-Compassion

Prayer: "Jesus, I can be hard on myself. Help me to practice self-compassion and to treat myself with the same love I offer to others."

Scripture Reference: "Love your neighbor as yourself." —Matthew 22:39

Contemplation: Why are you so mean to yourself sometimes?

Daily Reminder: "I will treat myself with love and compassion; I am worthy."

Engaging Prompt: Write a self-compassion letter, offering yourself understanding and kindness. How does it feel to extend this love to yourself?

My Tender Prayer: "Dear God, thank You for the opportunities that lie ahead. Help me to approach them with an open mind and heart. Amen."

Reflection Prompt: What opportunities are you looking forward to? Reflect on how you can prepare to embrace them.

December 13: God, Help Me to Honor My Growth

Prayer: "Hey God, growth is wild and messy, but it's also so beautiful. Help me honor every awkward stumble and every little victory along the way. Remind me to celebrate the amazing, ever-evolving person I'm becoming—flaws, sparkle, and all. Amen."

Scripture Reference: "But grow in the grace and knowledge of our Lord and Savior Jesus Christ." —2 Peter 3:18

Contemplation: In what ways have you grown this year? How can you acknowledge and celebrate this growth?

Daily Reminder: "I will honor my growth; it is part of my journey."

Engaging Prompt: Reflect on how you've changed this year. Write down three ways you can celebrate this growth in December.

My Tender Prayer: "God, I thank You for the beauty in the everyday, the little moments that remind me of Your love. Help me to embrace each day with a heart full of gratitude, finding joy in both the big and small blessings You've placed in my life. Teach me to see Your presence in the most unexpected ways. Amen."

Reflection Prompt: What are three moments today that made you feel grateful? Reflect on how God's love shines through these blessings and how you can carry that gratitude with you in the days ahead.

December 14: God, Help Me to Forgive Myself

Prayer: "Jesus, forgiving others can be hard, but forgiving myself is even harder. Help me to release guilt and embrace your forgiveness."

Scripture Reference: "If we confess our sins, he is faithful and just and will forgive us our sins." —1 John 1:9

Contemplation: What burdens of guilt are you carrying? How can forgiveness free you to live fully?

Daily Reminder: "I am forgiven; I will release guilt."

Engaging Prompt: Write a letter to yourself offering forgiveness for past mistakes. How does this act of self-forgiveness change your perspective?

My Tender Prayer: "Lord, thank You for the beauty of fresh perspectives and the wisdom they bring. Help me embrace change with grace, trusting that every shift opens doors to deeper growth and self-discovery. Guide me to walk confidently into the unknown, knowing it's shaping me into the woman I'm meant to be. Amen."

Reflection Prompt: What new perspective have you gained this year? Reflect on how it has changed your outlook.

December 15: God, Help Me to Find Peace in Silence

Prayer: "Hey God, in our busy lives, silence can be hard to find. Help me to seek peace in moments of stillness and to listen for your guidance."

Scripture Reference: "Be still and know that I am God." —Psalm 46:10

Contemplation: What distractions keep you from finding peace? How can you incorporate silence into your daily routine?

Daily Reminder: "Peace is found in stillness; I will seek it."

Engaging Prompt: Set aside ten minutes for silence today. What thoughts or feelings arise during this time?

My Tender Prayer: "Heavenly Father, may I radiate my unique love and compassion toward myself and others. Teach me to be gentle in my interactions. Amen."

Reflection Prompt: How can you show compassion to yourself today? Write about one way to practice self-love.

December 16: God, Help Me to Trust in Your Plan

Prayer: "Jesus, trust can be challenging, especially when I don't see the path ahead. Help me to trust in your divine plan for my life."

Scripture Reference: "The Lord will fight for you; you need only to be still." —Exodus 14:14

Contemplation: How can you cultivate trust in God's timing? What steps can you take to lean into faith?

Daily Reminder: "I will trust in God's plan; it is for my good."

Engaging Prompt: Reflect on a time when trust led to unexpected blessings in your life. How can you apply this perspective moving forward?

My Tender Prayer: "Lord, thank You for guiding me on this beautiful journey of growth. Help me to recognize and celebrate the steps I've taken, the lessons I've learned, and the person I am becoming. May I always honor the progress I've made with grace and gratitude. Amen."

Reflection Prompt: Take a moment to reflect on the growth you've experienced this year. What are the moments that stand out as your biggest achievements? How can you carry this growth forward into the next chapter of your life?

December 17: God, Help Me to Celebrate My Unique Journey

Prayer: "Hey God, my journey is a wild mix of twists, turns, and a few unexpected detours, but it's all mine. Help me figure out what I truly want and celebrate every chapter—messy moments included. Show me how to see the beauty in the chaos and embrace my story as it unfolds. Amen."

Scripture Reference: "For I am the Lord your God, who takes hold of your right hand and says to you, do not fear; I will help you." —Isaiah 41:13

Contemplation: What makes your journey unique? How can you embrace your individuality as part of your story?

Daily Reminder: "My story is mine alone; I will celebrate it."

Engaging Prompt: Write about a moment that defined your journey this year. How does this moment shape your perspective?

My Tender Prayer: "Lord, thank You for the power of forgiveness. Help me to release any lingering resentments and embrace a sense of peace. Amen."

Reflection Prompt: What ways do you feel free from your past?

December 18: God, Help Me to Cultivate Joy

Prayer: "Jesus, joy is a gift I want to embrace. Help me to find joy in the ordinary and to celebrate the little things in life."

Scripture Reference: "Rejoice in the Lord always. I will say it again: Rejoice!" —Philippians 4:4

Contemplation: What brings you joy? How can you invite more joy into your daily life?

Daily Reminder: "Joy is found in the little things; I will celebrate them."

Engaging Prompt: List five things that bring you joy. How can you incorporate more of these into your life?

My Tender Prayer: "Dear God, help me to be present in each moment. Teach me to find beauty in the now, rather than the past or future. Amen."

Reflection Prompt: What does it mean to be present to you? Write about how you can practice mindfulness today.

December 19: God, Help Me to Embrace Community

Prayer: Hey God, community is a vital part of my journey. Help me to embrace and nurture the relationships around me, knowing I'm not alone."

Scripture Reference: "And let us consider how we may spur one another on toward love and good deeds." —Hebrews 10:24

Contemplation: Who in your life serves as your support system? How can you strengthen these connections?

Daily Reminder: "I am part of a community; I will nurture it."

Engaging Prompt: Reach out to someone in your community today. How can you support each other on your journeys?

My Tender Prayer: "God, may I recognize the pervasiveness of my thoughts. Help me to cultivate a positive mindset that uplifts myself and others. Amen."

Reflection Prompt: What negative thought patterns do you want to change? Write about how you can shift your perspective.

December 20: God, Help Me to Learn from My Relationships

Prayer: "Jesus, relationships teach me so much. Help me to learn from my past relationships and to embrace the growth they've inspired. I do know more about what I want and deserve in relationships through past experiences and for that I am thankful I can recognize the distinction."

Scripture Reference: "As iron sharpens iron, so one person sharpens another." —Proverbs 27:17

Contemplation: What have your relationships taught you this year? How can you apply these lessons moving forward?

Daily Reminder: "I will learn from my relationships; they are part of my growth."

Engaging Prompt: Reflect on a relationship that taught you an important lesson. How has this shaped your perspective on love and connection?

My Tender Prayer: "Lord, thank You for the beauty of nature. Help me to appreciate its wonders and find peace in the world around me. Amen."

Reflection Prompt: Spend time outside today or even at a window. Write or sketch something in nature that inspires you.

December 21: God, Help Me to Find My Voice

Prayer: "Hey God, finding my voice can be a journey. Help me to speak my truth and to share my story with confidence."

Scripture Reference: "Let your conversation be always full of grace, seasoned with salt, so that you may know how to answer everyone." —Colossians 4:6

Contemplation: What prevents you from speaking your truth? How can you cultivate confidence in sharing your story?

Daily Reminder: "My voice matters; I will share it."

Engaging Prompt: Write a letter to someone expressing your thoughts and feelings. How does this act of sharing your voice empower you?

My Tender Prayer: "Heavenly Father, help me embrace the unknown with courage. Teach me to trust in Your guidance as I step into new possibilities. Amen."

Reflection Prompt: What fears do you have about the unknown? Write about how you can find peace in uncertainty.

December 22: God, Help Me to Recognize My Strengths

Prayer: "Jesus, I want to recognize and celebrate my strengths. Help me to see the unique gifts you've given me and to embrace them fully."

Scripture Reference: "We have different gifts, according to the grace given to each of us." —Romans 12:6

Contemplation: What are your strengths? How can you use them to serve others and your community?

Daily Reminder: "I will celebrate my strengths; they are a part of who I am."

Engaging Prompt: List three strengths you possess. How can you apply these gifts in your daily life?

My Tender Prayer: "God, may I honor the cycles of life. Help me to accept the seasons of my journey with grace and gratitude. Amen."

Reflection Prompt: Reflect on a cycle in your life. What does it teach you about growth and change?

December 22: God, Help Me to Recognize My Strengths

Prayer: "Jesus, I want to recognize and celebrate my strengths. Help me to see the unique gifts you've given me and to embrace them fully."

Scripture Reference: "We have different gifts, according to the grace given to each of us." —Romans 12:6

Contemplation: What are your strengths? How can you use them to serve others and your community?

Daily Reminder: "I will celebrate my strengths; they are a part of who I am."

Engaging Prompt: List three strengths you possess. How can you apply these gifts in your daily life?

My Tender Prayer: "God, may I honor the cycles of life. Help me to accept the seasons of my journey with grace and gratitude. Amen."

Reflection Prompt: Reflect on a cycle in your life. What does it teach you about growth and change?

December 23: God, Help Me to Seek Balance

Prayer: "Hey God, balance can be elusive in today's world. Help me to find balance in my life and to prioritize what truly matters."

Scripture Reference: "A time for everything, and a season for every activity under the heavens." —Ecclesiastes 3:1

Contemplation: What areas of your life feel out of balance? How can you prioritize self-care and wellness?

Daily Reminder: "I will seek balance; it brings peace to my soul."

Engaging Prompt: Reflect on your daily routine. What adjustments can you make to create more balance in your life?

My Tender Prayer: "Lord, thank You for the gift of creativity. Help me to express myself freely and explore my passions. Amen."

Reflection Prompt: What creative pursuits inspire you? Plan time to engage in one of them today.

December 24: God, Help Me to Appreciate My Growth

Prayer: "Jesus, growth is a journey that can be both challenging and beautiful. Help me to appreciate how far I've come, even on the tough days. May I find strength in each step and embrace the lessons learned. Amen."

Scripture Reference: "Being confident of this, that he who began a good work in you will carry it on to completion." —Philippians 1:6

Contemplation: How can you show encouragement to a friend?

Daily Reminder: "I will appreciate my growth; it is a beautiful journey."

Engaging Prompt Write a letter to your future self. What advice would you give about your journey and growth?

My Tender Prayer "Dear God, as this year fades into the next, help me to reflect on my journey with an open heart and a soul full of grace. May I embrace every part of who I am—each moment, each lesson, each experience—as a sacred step toward my truest, most sensual self. Guide me to honor my feminine essence and the strength that lies within my vulnerability. Amen."

Reflection Prompt: What are your goals for the next year?

December 25: God, Help Me to Embrace My Uniqueness

Prayer: "Hey God, I want to embrace my uniqueness and to celebrate the person you created me to be. Help me to let go of comparisons and to love who I am."

Scripture Reference: "For we are God's handiwork, created in Christ Jesus to do good works." —Ephesians 2:10

Contemplation: Just be yourself, don't ever think it.

Daily Reminder: "I will embrace my uniqueness; it is a gift."

Engaging Prompt: List three things that make you unique. How can you celebrate these aspects of yourself?

My Tender Prayer: "God, may I shine with the radiant light of my unique self. Help me to honor the essence of who I am—sensual, fierce, and unapologetically authentic. Guide me to embrace my individuality and celebrate every curve, every thought, every whisper of my soul. Let me step into the world with a heart full of wonder, knowing that my true self is a gift to this world. Amen."

Reflection Prompt: What are the qualities that make you uniquely you? How can you embrace and share these traits with the world in a way that feels bold, beautiful, and full of confidence?

December 26: God, Help Me to Set Intentions for the New Year

Prayer: "Jesus, as this year fades into the newness ahead of us, I want to set intentions for the new year. Help me to think creatively about the life I want to live."

Scripture Reference: "Delight yourself in the Lord, and He will give you the desires of your heart." —Psalm 37:4

Contemplation: What will be important to you in the new year?

Daily Reminder: "I will set intentions with purpose; they will guide my journey."

Engaging Prompt: Write down three intentions for the new year. How will you work toward these goals?

My Tender Prayer: "Lord, thank You for the love that surrounds me. Help me to appreciate the connections I have with others. Amen."

Reflection Prompt: Who do you feel connected to this season? Write about how you can strengthen those bonds.

December 27: God, Help Me to Rejoice in Your Faithfulness

Prayer: "Hey God, Your faithfulness is like the ultimate plot twist I can always count on. Help me to actually chill and trust that You've got it all handled. Teach me to celebrate Your promises, even when life feels like a reality television episode. Amen."

Scripture Reference: "The Lord is good, a refuge in times of trouble. He cares for those who trust in him." —Nahum 1:7

Contemplation: It all worked out so far, hasn't it?

Daily Reminder: "I will rejoice in God's faithfulness; it is my strength."

Engaging Prompt: Tell a friend how great they are doing at being themselves.

My Tender Prayer: "Heavenly Father, help me find joy in giving and receiving love. Teach me to appreciate the warmth of connection. Amen."

Reflection Prompt: What acts of kindness can you offer to others? Plan to do one kind act today.

December 28: God, Help Me to Seek Renewal

Prayer: "Jesus, renewal is a gift I want to embrace. Help me to seek renewal in my spirit, mind, and body as I prepare for the new year."

Scripture Reference: "Therefore we do not lose heart. Though outwardly we are wasting away, yet inwardly we are being renewed day by day." —2 Corinthians 4:16

Contemplation: What areas of your life feel in need of renewal? How can you intentionally nurture this process?

Daily Reminder: "I will seek renewal; it brings refreshment to my spirit."

Engaging Prompt: Plan a day of renewal for yourself. What activities will you include to refresh your spirit?

My Tender Prayer: "God, may I approach the new year with hope and excitement. Help me to set intentions that align with my wellbeing. Amen."

Reflection Prompt: Why does the New Year feel so important?

December 29: God, Help Me to Reflect on My Year

Prayer: "Hey God, Contemplation is an important part of growth. Help me to look back on this year with gratitude and understanding."

Scripture Reference: "Let all that I am praise the Lord; may I never forget the good things he does for me." —Psalm 103:2

Contemplation: Who do you want to see more in the new year?

Daily Reminder: "I will reflect with gratitude; it is part of my journey."

Engaging Prompt: Create a "Year in Review" collage or journal page. Include highlights, challenges, and lessons learned.

My Tender Prayer: "Lord, thank You for the journey of self-discovery. Help me to continue exploring who I am and who I am meant to be. Amen."

Reflection Prompt: What have you discovered about yourself this year? What have others discovered about you?

December 30: God, Help Me to Embrace the Future with Hope

Prayer: "Jesus, the future is filled with possibilities. Help me to embrace it with hope, knowing you are guiding my steps."

Scripture Reference: "Hope deferred makes the heart sick, but a longing fulfilled is a tree of life." —Proverbs 13:12

Contemplation: What hopes do you have for the future? How can you cultivate a mindset of hope as you step into the new year?

Daily Reminder: "I will embrace the future with hope; it is filled with promise."

Engaging Prompt: Write a letter to your future self, expressing your hopes and dreams for the coming year. What are you excited about?

My Tender Prayer: "Jesus, as this year fades into the next, help me reflect on the beauty of my journey with gratitude in my heart. May I feel your presence in every curve, every step, every whisper of growth, embracing the sensual grace of my becoming. Guide me into this new year with softness and strength, and may I step into all that I deserve with open arms and an open heart. Amen."

Reflection Prompt: Where are you spending New Year's Eve?

December 31: God, Help Me to Celebrate the Journey

Prayer: "Hey God, as we close out this month and step into the New Year, help me savor every step of this journey. Let me honor the woman I've become—the strength, the softness, the sensuality, and the lessons woven through each experience. May I celebrate how far I've come and look forward to all that's still to come, holding myself with love and gratitude. Amen."

Scripture Reference: "Let everything that has breath praise the Lord. Praise the Lord!" —Psalm 150:6

Contemplation: How can you celebrate the journey you've taken this year? What does honoring your growth mean to you?

Daily Reminder: "I will celebrate my journey; it is a testament to my growth."

Engaging Prompt: Check on all your friends.

My Tender Prayer: "God, thank You for this year of transformation and renewal. May I step into the New Year with confidence and faith. Amen."

Reflection Prompt: Love the journey going forward with faith.

Reflection

Reflection

As we reach the end of our journey through "JESUS LOVES ME AND MY BODY COUNT: A YEAR OF PRAYER AND SELF-REFLECTION FOR THE MODERN WOMAN," I hope you feel a renewed sense of purpose, empowerment, and connection to both yourself and your faith. This journal was designed to be a safe space—a sanctuary where you could explore the multifaceted aspects of your life without shame or judgment. It was created to celebrate your journey, recognizing that each twist and turn has led you to the beautiful person you are today.

Throughout the past year, you've engaged in heartfelt prayers, reflected on your experiences, and embraced your sensuality as part of your story. You've confronted the complexities of relationships, acknowledged your past, and emerged with a deeper understanding of what it means to be a woman of faith in today's world. You have taken the time to pause, reflect, and connect with the divine love that is always present, offering you grace and strength, no matter your circumstances and no matter your past. However, the journey doesn't end here. The lessons you've learned and the growth you've experienced can continue to guide you as you move forward. Your relationship with God is a living, breathing journey, and it will evolve as you do. Embrace that evolution, knowing that you are deserving of love, understanding, and redemption every step of the way.

As you close this journal, take a moment to reflect on your favorite insights, prayers, and art prompts. Consider keeping this book nearby as a source of inspiration and comfort—a reminder of the love and strength that resides within you.

Thank you for allowing me to accompany you on this path of self-discovery and spiritual growth. May you continue to walk boldly in your truth, with Jesus by your side, celebrating every part of who you are. Carry the knowledge that you are fearfully and wonderfully made, and that your body count does not define your value or worth to society, others or yourself. You are a beautiful, complex, and empowered woman, and you are loved unconditionally.

Here's to new beginnings, fierce faith, and a life filled with purpose and joy. Keep shining, keep loving, and always remember: Jesus loves you and so do I.

| 395 | – REFLECTION

What Can a Modern Woman Do?

What Can a Modern Woman Do?

As we wrap up this empowering journey together, I want to take a moment to reflect on all that we've explored over the past year. From embracing new beginnings and self-love to cultivating fierce faith and celebrating redemption, each month has been a testament to the strength and resilience that resides within us. We've laughed, cried, and reflected on our pasts, learning that every experience—no matter how spicy—contributes to the beautiful tapestry of our lives.

But this isn't the end; it's merely a steppingstone. The journey of growth, faith, and self-discovery is ongoing. I encourage you to take what you've learned here and carry it into your daily life. Reflect on the lessons, practice gratitude, and nurture your faith. Be bold in your intentions and courageous in your authenticity. Remember, your past is not a weight to carry; it's a foundation upon which you can build a brighter future.

Next, are some actionable steps to keep the momentum going:

1. Continue Journaling: Set aside time each week to reflect on your thoughts, prayers, and experiences. Use the prompts in this book or create your own.

2. Share Your Journey: Connect with friends, family, or a community that shares your values. Sharing your story can foster support and understanding.

3. Set Intentions: At the start of each month, write down specific intentions that align with the themes we've discussed. Hold yourself accountable and celebrate your progress.

4. Practice Gratitude: Each day, take a moment to express gratitude for the blessings in your life, no matter how small. Cultivating gratitude can shift your perspective and invite joy.

5. Embrace Your Faith: Whether you're returning to church or exploring your spirituality, find ways to deepen your connection with God. Seek community, read scripture, and engage in prayer.

6. Celebrate Your Growth: Acknowledge how far you've come and the lessons you've learned. Treat yourself to moments of joy and Contemplation as you continue your journey.

Your story is far from over, and the path ahead is filled with possibility. Embrace it with an open heart and a fierce spirit. Let's continue to walk this journey of faith, self-love, and empowerment together.

With love and determination,

THANK YOU FOR TAKING THIS JOURNALING YEAR
Amber Chase

ANGELFACEBADDIES.COM

DJKITTYMITTENS.COM

www.ingramcontent.com/pod-product-compliance
Lightning Source LLC
Chambersburg PA
CBHW060416010526
44107CB00006B/713